In Touch
with the Word

Lectionary-Based
Prayer Reflections

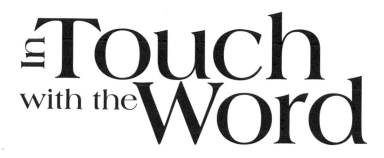

In Touch with the Word

Lectionary-Based Prayer Reflections

Cycle B for Ordinary Time

Lisa-Marie Calderone-Stewart

Saint Mary's Press
Christian Brothers Publications
Winona, Minnesota

Thank you, Mom, for the weekly fun and encouragement.
No matter what happens in my life, my first thought is always,
"I can't wait to tell Mom about this!"
Here's one more book to put in the trunk of your car!

Thank you, Ralph, for the daily fun and encouragement.
You help me dream my dreams, yet keep my feet on the ground.
You inspire my creative juices!

Thank you, Bishop Ken Untener.
You have had a major influence
on my spiritual formation, my ministry, and my life.

  Genuine recycled paper with 10% post-consumer
waste. Printed with soy-based ink.

The publishing team for this book included Robert P. Stamschror,
development editor; Laurie A. Berg, copy editor; Lynn Dahdal,
production editor; Hollace Storkel, typesetter; Stephan Nagel and
Kent Linder, cover designers; Maurine R. Twait, art director; pre-
press, printing, and binding by the graphics division of Saint
Mary's Press.

The acknowledgments continue on page 146.

Printed in the United States of America

Printing: 9 8 7 6 5 4 3 2 1

Year: 2007 06 05 04 03 02 01 00 99

ISBN 0-88489-577-7, paper
ISBN 0-88489-578-5, spiral

I dedicate this book to:

Fr. Robert P. Stamschror,
Recipient of the 1998
NFCYM
(National Federation for Catholic Youth Ministry)
National Youth Ministry Award
In the category of Publisher/Author/Artist

You had faith in me as a writer
Long before I was an author.

Your critical eye and your challenge for excellence
Have made books out of my manuscripts.

I never call you "Father Bob,"
But in many ways
You have become a father figure for me.

You look at my accomplishments with pride
and affection,
Knowing that your hands
Are the ones that have taught and guided me
along the way.

You are a joy to work with
And a delight to be with.

Having you as my editor has been a blessing.
Having you as my friend has been an honor.

Thank you for enriching my life.

Contents

Introduction

Did you ever go to Mass on Sunday, listen to the Scripture readings, and then promptly forget what they were all about or how your life relates to their message? Does this sound familiar? Even though you may have listened to a homilist who connected the word with you and challenged you at that time, what about the week before the Sunday Scriptures or the week after? How can you anticipate and prepare for the word? How can you stay in touch with the word that was heard?

This book is a resource designed to do just that—to help you prepare for the Sunday Scripture readings and to help you stay in touch with the word.

Using This Book

Using *In Touch with the Word* is a simple procedure. First, decide which Sunday's readings you are going to share. If it is Friday afternoon, you might want to reflect on the readings for the next Sunday so you can be more prepared for the upcoming liturgy. If it is Monday morning, you might want to remember the readings you heard on Sunday so you can stay in touch with that word the rest of the week. Next, turn to the page for the Sunday you have in mind. There you will find reflections, questions, and a prayer based on that Sunday's readings.

The Sunday Scripture Readings

The Scripture readings for each Sunday are found in a book called a lectionary. The Sunday readings follow a three-year, A-B-C cycle that continues to repeat itself. The readings in the A cycle highlight the Gospel of Matthew. The readings in the B cycle highlight the Gospel of Mark. The readings in the C cycle highlight the Gospel of Luke. (If you are wondering about the Gospel of John, don't be concerned. His readings are woven throughout all three years on special days that seem to need that "John" touch.)

The church calendar year consists of the seasons of Advent and Christmas, Lent and Easter, plus Ordinary Time. This book covers Ordinary Time, B cycle only. (The Sundays of A and C cycle in Ordinary Time, and the Sundays of the Advent, Christmas, Lent, and Easter seasons will be found in other volumes of this series.) Most Sundays have three sets of readings, one for each cycle. But in this book you will only find the readings for the B cycle. The dates for each Sunday in the B cycle are given for the next several years.

You will note that the Scripture readings are not reprinted in this book. It would make the book too big and too expensive. You will need either a lectionary or a Bible to read one or more of the Scripture readings as part of the prayer reflection. However, a capsulated version of each Scripture reading is provided.

One (and possibly two) of the three Scripture readings listed with each Sunday has an open bullet (○) next to it. This indicates which reading will be most focused on in the reflection and which one you might want to read as part of the reflection.

Theme

A summary of a central theme of the readings is also offered. You may want to use it to set a context for the reflection questions that will initiate sharing of and reflection on the word.

Reflection Questions

The reflection questions for each Sunday address audiences in three categories: adults, teenagers, and children. However, feel free to cross categories in the use of the questions whenever it is appropriate.

Focusing Object

For each set of readings, you will find a suggested focusing object. Using a focusing object in these prayer reflections is not mandatory, but it is helpful, especially with teenagers and children. It is a visual, hands-on reminder of the readings and their message. For example, anticipating or recalling the meaning of the passage about our relationship with Jesus being like a vine and its branches is much easier and more vivid if a plant with a stem and branches is present when reflecting on the reading of that passage.

The focusing object is handy for facilitating the prayer reflection and sharing. For example, after the Scripture reading is proclaimed, the facilitator asks one of the reflection questions for everyone to think about and share their thoughts. Then the facilitator picks up the focusing object and begins the sharing. When finished, the facilitator passes the object to the next person who is ready to share.

The focusing object can be passed around a circle, so everyone knows when their turn is coming, or it can be passed randomly as people become ready to share. A large group does better sitting in a circle and passing the object around in order. In a small group—one that fits around a table where everyone can reach the middle—anyone who is ready can pick up the object, share, and replace it for the next person who is ready to take a turn. Also, using the object makes it obvious when a person's turn has ended—no one has to guess. If someone just wants to offer a one-word response, or even remain silent, the focusing object is simply handed to the next person.

The focusing object is more than a reminder or a turn-designator. It is also an effective way to reduce the self-conscious feeling many people get when they are expected to share with a group of their peers. Persons handling an object and looking at it tend to relax and forget that a roomful of people are watching them. People who are relaxed and comfortable do a better job of sharing. This is true of adults, teenagers, and children!

After everyone has had a chance to share, the object comes back to the facilitator, who ends with the "Closing" or any other words she or he feels would be appropriate.

The focusing object can stay on a kitchen table or a classroom shelf all week, acting as a reminder of God's word and the people's response.

Closing

A closing is provided for each prayer reflection. It consists of a poem or reading that ends the reflections with an inspirational touch. You will notice that the closings come from a variety of cultures and each culture adds a rich spiritual tradition to the prayer reflections.

Indexes

Each Sunday's prayer session is indexed by focusing object and by theme in the back of this book.

Settings

Parish

Parish staffs, councils, and committees usually want to start their meetings with some type of prayer. Prayer based on Sunday's readings is a great way to help the group relate to the parish liturgy, connect with the message of the Sunday readings, and start the meeting off on a spiritual plane.

Homilists can benefit from this resource by looking at the message through the eyes of adults, teenagers, and children. This can provide a springboard for the type of insights needed to be pastoral, effective, and challenging to the assembly of mixed ages that typically gathers each Sunday. (Actually sharing the reflection questions with adults, teenagers, and children and listening to their responses each week provides even better feedback for a homilist!)

Liturgy planning groups will find this book helpful. Members with different degrees of liturgical experience and understanding can read the theme summaries, share the questions, and get a feel for the flow of the Scriptures. The suggested focusing object can also remind the group to investigate the possibilities of symbolism in the physical environment of the worship space.

Prayer groups and small Christian communities will find *In Touch with the Word* very helpful, especially if the groups include families with children of different ages.

Youth
Groupings

Youth ministers will find the prayer reflections in this book a simple way to prepare a youth group or team for the readings they will hear the following Sunday or feast day and to help them stay in touch with the readings they heard the previous Sunday. At the same time, the reflections call attention to the major seasons of the church year. The prayer process in the reflections works equally well with junior high teens or high school teens.

Parish religious education teachers and catechists meeting with a class once a week can use this resource to relate to the Sunday and feast day readings. Sending a note home each week encouraging parents to discuss the readings with their children at the dinner table or at bedtime, perhaps with a similar focusing object, is a good way to weave a family connection into a parish religious education program.

Religion teachers in Catholic schools looking for a way to connect students with their parish community will value this resource. Anticipating or recalling the Scriptures read at the parish liturgies will help students stay in touch with their parish community.

Families

Busy families will find that using *In Touch with the Word* at home is a great way to make liturgical worship more relevant for their teenagers or younger children. Using the prayer reflections does not take long and is easy to do. Best of all, it helps the family as a whole connect with what is said at Mass and remember it throughout the week. Parents may find their teenagers more likely to share prayer if they are doing it "for the sake of their younger brothers and sisters" than if they think they are doing it for themselves!

Parishes with family-based programming can use this resource in several ways. If the parish supplies families with resources to be used at home, every family can receive a copy of *In Touch with the Word* to use on their own. If families gather regularly at the parish for a scheduled activity, the sharing process can be incorporated with the program. If family groups meet in cells or units, they can be provided with copies of this book and suggestions for how it can be used in the context of their meeting.

Whether you work with adults, teenagers, or children in a parish, school, or home setting, you will find that being in touch with the word is easy with *In Touch with the Word*.

Trinity Sunday

18 June 2000
15 June 2003
11 June 2006

Baptism

Scripture

- *Deuteronomy 4:32–34,39–40.* Moses questions the people, "Has anything as great as this ever happened before?" in order to help them see the awesome greatness of their God.
- *Romans 8:14–17.* We are children of God: created by our *Abba,* heirs with Christ, and led by the Spirit. We have been chosen because of great love.
- *Matthew 28:16–20.* From a great mountaintop, Jesus commissions the disciples to go forth and baptize in the name of God as Trinity.

Theme

Great things happen on mountaintops, and all three readings revolve around the greatness of God and God's love. Moses calls the Israelites to consider the great things done by God, and Paul challenges the Romans to consider the greatness of our Christian heritage. Finally, the conclusion of Matthew's Gospel has Jesus on top of a mountain, sending forth the eleven chosen ones to do great things—to baptize and to teach, and to know that he will be with them until the end of the world.

Focusing Object
A shell (as used to pour water in baptism)

Reflections

The eleven Apostles Jesus chose (minus Judas) are thrust into greatness at the moment of this commissioning. They are sent forth to baptize in the name of God as Trinity, and to teach and carry out the mission of faith Jesus showed them with his life. They are hardly great individuals. They didn't yet exhibit great courage, great understanding, or even great faith. But Jesus believes in them, and that's all that matters.

- What do you think it must have been like for the eleven Apostles at that moment?
- When have you ever felt thrust into a position where you felt inadequate to do what you had to do? Who was depending on you? Where or how did you find the courage and ability to do what had to be done?

When we are baptized, we are reborn into greatness. Most of us are infants and have no idea of the significance of the moment. Most of us cry and fuss and just want to be held and comforted. Some who are adults at baptism later report that they still didn't fully comprehend the grace of the sacrament at the time; it's an awareness that we slowly grow into as our faith matures.

- What's your knowledge of your own baptism? How do you view that moment?
- When was the most recent baptism you have witnessed? How did you feel witnessing that event?
- Are you a godmother or a godfather? If so, how do you view your role as a mentor in faith for your godchild?
- What does it mean to be baptized in the name of the Father, *Abba,* our Creator, our Mother, our Source of Being?
- What does it mean to be baptized in the name of the Son, the Christ, our Savior, our Redeemer, our Teacher, our Brother?
- What does it mean to be baptized in the name of the Holy Spirit, the Sanctifier, the One who makes

all things holy, the Breath and Wind of change and growth?

For Teenagers
The twelve Apostles are not great people. At the time Jesus commissions them, only eleven remain, because one has committed suicide after betraying Jesus. Peter denies Jesus, Thomas doubts that he has risen, and none of them really understand what Jesus was all about. But they became great because Jesus sent them forth to do great things. They were given a responsibility, and they lived up to it.

- When have you been given a big job to do? When did someone believe in you? When did you live up to a responsibility, even though you were not necessarily confident in your abilities?
- How is it that ordinary people can end up doing great things?

When we are baptized, it is done in the name of God as Trinity. We are baptized in the name of a God that has relationship and love as the inner core: "Father, Son, and Holy Spirit."

- *"Father . . ."* Think of your father, your mother, your grandparents. Think of life, think of being created. Think of the times you have been creative and you have formed something out of an idea. This is what our *Abba* is about. What kind of God is this? Why are we baptized in the name of this God? What does it mean?
- *". . . Son . . ."* Think of yourself as a son or a daughter. Think of yourself as a brother or a sister. Think of yourself as a teacher or a student of another. Think of yourself as a friend. This is what Jesus is about. What kind of God is this? Why are we baptized in the name of this God? What does it mean?
- *". . . Holy Spirit."* Think of holiness. Think of power. Think of energy. Think of goodness. Think of the positive force of doing the right thing just because it's the right thing to do. Think of the joy that comes to you when you make the right decision. Think of the harmony of all people

joining together to be a support to one another. Think of love. This is what the Holy Spirit is all about. What kind of God is this? Why are we baptized in the name of this God? What does it mean?

For Children

When we bless ourselves, we make the sign of the cross and say, "Father, Son, and Holy Spirit. Amen." We call that the Trinity. The Trinity is one God that is three persons, the Father, the Son, and the Holy Spirit.

- God the Father is sometimes called *Abba*. *Abba* is like our father, our mother, or our grandparents. We are here because our family loves us and takes care of us. How does your family take care of you? How does *Abba* take care of you?
- God the Son is Jesus. Jesus is like our brother, our teacher, or our best friend. Do you have any brothers or sisters? What are their names? What is the name of your teacher? What does your teacher teach you about? Who is one of your best friends? What does he or she like to do? What do you know about Jesus?
- God the Holy Spirit is the part of God that lives inside of us. Every time you take care of someone or help someone or do something good, you are working with God to make the world better. When have you done something special for someone?

In the Gospel story, Jesus tells his Apostles to go out and baptize people.

- Have you ever seen someone get baptized? If so, what happens?

Closing

Be not afraid of greatness: some are born great, some achieve greatness, and some have greatness thrust upon them. —William Shakespeare

(Go for the Gold)

Feast of the Body and Blood of Christ

25 June 2000
22 June 2003
18 June 2006

Passover
and
Eucharist

Scripture

- *Exodus 24:3–8.* Moses seals the Covenant between Israel and God with the blood of a sacrifice.
- *Hebrews 9:11–15.* The old covenant of atoning for sins with the blood of sacrificed animals is compared to the new Covenant of atoning for sins for all time with the blood of Jesus—the perfect sacrifice.
- *Mark 14:12–16,22–26.* Jesus instructs two of his disciples to go into the city to prepare the group's Passover meal. The disciples find everything just as he predicted. There, Jesus shares his Last Supper, which becomes our eucharistic feast.

Theme

The story of Moses in Exodus describes the *old* covenant, sealed with the blood of a sacrifice. The story of Jesus in Mark's Gospel describes the start of the *new* Covenant; after the meal the group goes to the Mount of Olives, where Jesus is prepared to seal the Covenant between people and God with his own blood, the blood of a perfect sacrifice. The explanation in the letter to the Hebrews compares the high priest of the old covenant to Jesus, who is the new high priest of the new Covenant.

Focusing Object
A cluster of grapes and a shaft of wheat

Reflections

This feast used to be called *Corpus Christi,* which is Latin for "Body of Christ." Yet now it is translated as not only the body but "the body *and blood* of Christ." The readings in this cycle really emphasize the blood, something that we are sometimes hesitant to accept and reflect upon. It is easier to image Jesus' body as bread. But to think about drinking Jesus' blood as we drink red wine might be too graphic for us to be comfortable with.

- Many people receive Communion weekly, even daily, in both forms—the bread and the wine, the body and the blood of Jesus. However, many people never receive from the cup. If you receive from the cup regularly, reflect on the completeness of your eucharistic experience. Do you remember the first time you received from the cup? If you do not receive from the cup regularly, reflect on the reasons for your choice. Might there be an issue of hygiene? Might there be an awkwardness with actually holding the cup?
- It might be interesting to stretch the imagination a bit and picture Jesus at the Last Supper, offering the bread as his body and the wine as his blood. What would Jesus say to his disciples if some of them ate the bread but said, "no, thank you" to the cup?

Jesus describes a very specific setting that his two disciples will encounter in the city. It must have been astonishing for them to discover everything that Jesus foretold.

- When those two disciples set out for the city, do you think they thoroughly trusted Jesus and believed that things would be exactly as Jesus had predicted, or do you think they might have had a "Let's wait and see how this whole thing happens" attitude?
- What would your attitude have been if you were given such a descriptive prediction of what you were going to find?

- How would you feel when things turned out exactly as they were described? Would you feel eerie? trusting? frightened by the power? Would you be more drawn to the person who made the prediction (from admiration or awe)? Or would you be driven away from that person (from fear or a haunting sense)?

There is a lot of talk about blood in these readings. Blood was mysterious in the days before biology and an understanding of life functions. People would be sprinkled with the blood of sacrificed animals; people would sign important documents in blood.

- Do you become upset or feel that you might faint at the sight of someone's heavy bleeding?
- When you were a small child, how did you react when you hurt yourself and then saw blood? Did seeing the blood make you feel more afraid and cry louder? Or did it distract you, bring out your curiosity, and calm you down?
- What do you think is the connection between the age-old human fascination with blood and Jesus' telling us that the bread and wine we receive in his name are actually his true body and blood?

For Children

When Jesus died on the cross, it was painful for him. The wounds from the nails really hurt, and he was bleeding while he died.

- Did you ever hurt yourself and bleed? How did it happen? What did you do? What's a good thing to do whenever anyone hurts themselves and starts to bleed?

When we go to Mass and receive Communion, we are not eating just ordinary bread and wine. We are actually receiving Jesus, because the bread is really his body and the wine is really his blood, even though it looks and tastes like regular bread and wine.

- If you are old enough to receive Communion, share what it's like to walk up in the line with everyone and receive Communion. Do you receive from both the bread and the cup? If not, why not? Do you remember the day of your First Communion? What was that day like? Were you nervous? happy? afraid? proud? How did you feel?

- If you are not old enough to receive Communion, share what it's like to walk up in the line with everyone and not receive. (Or share what it's like to stay in your seat and wait for everyone else to come back.) How do you feel at Communion time? When do you think you will receive your First Communion?

Closing

When the Creator gives you something, don't hesitate. Grab it. —A Native American Elder
(Native Wisdom for White Minds)

Second Sunday of the Year

16 January 2000
19 January 2003
15 January 2006

We Are Called

Scripture

- ○ *1 Samuel 3:3–10,19.* God calls Samuel while Samuel sleeps. At first he doesn't recognize God's call, but Eli eventually helps Samuel to understand and respond.
- • *1 Corinthians 6:13–15,17–20.* Paul reminds us that our bodies are a temple for the Holy Spirit.
- • *John 1:35–42.* Jesus asks, "What are you looking for?" and invites curious passersby to "come and see" what he is about. They become his disciples.

Theme

We are being called. Sometimes we don't realize it at first. Like Samuel we are asleep, or we need someone wise to help us discern our calling. Sometimes we do realize it, and we must change our life, as Paul suggests, to reflect the holiness of our call. Sometimes it is more obvious, as if Jesus is boldly asking us what we're looking for. What are we being called to? Discipleship.

Focusing Object

A telephone

Reflections

Jesus is calling us to be his disciples. Every one of us is called. How we hear the call and how we respond is what makes us unique.

- How have you been called to follow Jesus? Has your call come at a sleepy time of your life?
- Like Samuel, did you need an Eli to help you figure out what God wanted you to do? Like Andrew, did you immediately hear Jesus asking you to "come and see"? Like Paul, did you know what behavior changes the Holy Spirit required of you?

Because of Eli's guidance, Samuel's response to God is, "Speak to me. I am your servant, and I am listening."

- Do you think God speaks to you? When? In what ways? How do you know?
- How are you a servant to God? How are you a servant to other gods (money, fame, work, cultural expectations, and so on)?
- Are you listening? Many people try to hear God's word, but insist that God seems silent when they pray. When you listen, what does God say?

Samuel is a young person, living with Eli, who is his spiritual guide. Samuel is inexperienced, and he needs Eli to walk with him and experience life with him so he is not alone.

- Who is a spiritual guide for you? Who is an adult with life experience whom you can trust and open up to when you have deep questions of the heart? How does this take place? When has this helped you?

God calls Samuel as God calls each of us. Samuel needs Eli's help to understand God's call, and Eli helps Samuel to listen and be open to what God has to say.

- Do you think you really listen to God? Do you think you are open to what God has to say to you? How can you improve in this area?

In the Gospel Jesus asks the curious passersby what they are looking for.

- What are you looking for in life? What do you think most teenagers your age are looking for?
- Do you think Jesus is the answer to everything most people are looking for? If not, why not? If so, why? And if so, why don't most teenagers realize that Jesus is the answer?

In the Gospel Jesus invites curious ones to "come and see" what his life is all about.

- What do you think Jesus' life is all about?
- If you invited a complete stranger to "come and see" what your life is all about, what would they think about you and your values and priorities after following you around for a week?

For Children

God calls upon Samuel while Samuel is sleeping. Samuel wakes up confused and thinks that Eli is calling him. At first Eli thinks Samuel is dreaming.

- Did you ever have a dream, and then wake up thinking that your dream was real? What was that like?
- Do you ever dream about God? What are those dreams like?

In the Gospel story, some people see Jesus and are curious about him. Jesus invites them to spend some time with him so they can get to know him.

- If you could invite Jesus to spend a day with you, what kinds of things would you like to show Jesus? What would you want to do with Jesus?
- If Jesus came to your house or to your school today, and he invited you to spend the day with him, what kinds of things do you think Jesus would want to show you and do with you?

Closing

God is much more anxious to communicate with us than we are to listen. —Morton Kelsey

(Action 2000: C Cycle)

Third Sunday of the Year

23 January 2000
26 January 2003
22 January 2006

Answering the Call

Scripture

- *Jonah 3:1–5,10.* The people of Nineveh respond immediately to Jonah's call to conversion and change in their lives.
- *1 Corinthians 7:29–31.* Paul challenges us to take nothing for granted, and to realize that change can happen quickly, for the world as we know it is passing.
- *Mark 1:14–20.* Right after John's arrest, Jesus shows up preaching. He walks by the Sea of Galilee, calls out to some of the fishermen, and they immediately follow him. Their lives would never be the same again.

Theme

Things can happen so quickly. "What a difference a day makes—24 little hours," as the song goes. Nineveh changes overnight because of Jonah's preaching. Simon, Andrew, James, and John immediately abandon their fishing nets to become fishers of men and women. Paul tells us to be prepared because these things can happen. He exaggerates the point so we know how urgent it is to be ready to alter our life completely for God.

Focusing Object

A fish, or a picture of a fish

Reflections

For Adults

Jesus sweeps through the Sea of Galilee, and leaves several empty fishing boats in his wake. People who had spent their life fishing abandoned their career and even their family members to change their life and follow this amazing Master who called them.

- What is the most drastic change that ever occurred in your life? What completely turned your existence upside down, so that you were never the same again?

At the time the Apostles first start to follow Jesus, they don't really understand what he is about or where he eventually will lead them. For a while their personal habits and thought patterns are challenged, but remain basically unchanged. Jesus wonders if anything he has said or done has ever gotten through to them. But eventually they catch on. And so does much of the world. The spread of Christianity is a remarkable example of what a small number of dedicated people can do. They truly became fishers of men and women.

- When are your personal habits and thought patterns basically unchanged and unaffected by the message of Jesus? When do you act as if his influence has hardly touched you?
- When have your decisions and behaviors been directly based on the message of Jesus?
- What can you do to be sure that your life is more deliberately based on Jesus—in action, and not only in word or intention? How can you be a fisher of people for a more faithful life?

For Teenagers

When Jesus comes by, the fishers who choose to follow him are immediately changed. Their daily lives are no longer spent watching the weather, fixing their boats, and hauling fish. Yet it takes them several years to understand their faith in Jesus and what it means to be a true follower and disciple.

Some changes can happen quickly, and things are immediately different. Some changes happen more slowly, and you can only see the difference over time, while looking back with a thoughtful eye.

- When you made the switch from junior high to high school (or from elementary school to junior high or middle school), what were the immediate changes in your everyday life? What were the changes that took time as you matured and became more adultlike and more comfortable with your new surroundings?
- What are some of the immediate daily changes that might have taken place in the Apostles' lives and in the lives of their family members? What gradual changes do you think their family members would have noticed in them over the course of three years or so?
- When you want to change yourself, how do you get from the stage of "just thinking about it" to the stage of "actually doing it"? What are some changes you would like to make in your own life—changes that would make you a better person, changes that Jesus would approve of?
- If you truly live that way every day—making changes that Jesus would approve of, being a better person—how will that make you like the Apostles? How might you become like a fisher of other teenagers, looking for a better life?

For Children

When Jesus comes along, the fishers leave their nets in their boats and follow Jesus. It is the first day of a whole new life for them.

- When was a first day of a whole new life for you?
- Do you remember your first day of school?
- Did you ever move to a new house or a new city?
- Did you ever have a new baby born into your family?

When Jesus calls the first disciples, he tells them that they won't be catching fish to eat anymore, but they will be catching people. Every person they catch will learn about Jesus and will live a good life.

- Who has taught you about Jesus? What have you learned? What is Jesus like?

Closing

- What kinds of things do you try to do every day so that you live a good life?

When people hear us speak God's word, they marvel at its beauty and power; when they see what little impact it has on our daily lives, they laugh and poke fun at us. —A second-century Christian

(Action 2000: C Cycle)

Fourth Sunday of the Year

30 January 2000
2 February 2003
29 January 2006

Cleansing the Unclean Spirit

Scripture

- *Deuteronomy 18:15–20.* Moses explains that God will raise up another prophet for the people to listen to.
- *1 Corinthians 7:32–35.* Paul explains why he has chosen the celibate life.
- *Mark 1:21–28.* Jesus' reputation spreads as he teaches with authority and casts out unclean spirits.

Theme

Moses speaks of another prophet that God will raise up, and Paul speaks of being completely dedicated to the service of God. Then Jesus comes along, and people are amazed at his words and deeds. His first act of power in Mark's Gospel is to make clean the people with unclean spirits.

Focusing Object
Cleanser, or a cleaning utensil

Reflections

For Adults

It is significant that Jesus speaks with authority and that he cleans the unclean. Only one with wisdom and experience and knowledge can speak with authority. Only one with understanding can be trusted. Only one with a vision of the clean can cure the unclean.

- Do you know someone you can trust completely? How do you know you can?
- Do you know a wise person, whose general advice you respect? Why is that?
- Whom do you know that has a vision of the clean and the righteous? How does this person's vision affect yours?
- How do you think the trust, wisdom, and vision of Jesus was recognized by the people?

We most often gain wisdom and understanding when we work hard on a difficult task that challenges us and stretches us, or when we survive a tragedy and are able to grow through our grief, or when we somehow have an encounter with the Divine and Infinite.

- How have any of these possibilities affected your life and brought you wisdom and understanding?
- Where might these possibilities have entered Jesus' life and affected him?

For Teenagers

Jesus is teaching in the synagogue, and people are impressed with his sense of authority. Jesus is "real." He isn't preachy or arrogant or standoffish or "churchy." He speaks at their level, he makes sense, he believes in what he is saying, and he doesn't want to play games with prestige or status.

- Do you know any teachers at school who have that gift?
- Do you know any leaders in your community or your church who are like that?
- Describe an adult you can relate to, one who is "real."

Jesus cleaned the unclean. He recognized the unclean, he knew what clean and unclean were all about, and he took action and made a difference.

- Anytime we clean anything, we take those same steps. We have to recognize the need to clean, we have to know what clean looks like, and we have to take action so that the unclean becomes clean. What is something you have cleaned that took quite a bit of work?

- Anytime we have a personal problem we need to clean up, or a bad habit we need to cure, we take the same basic cleaning steps. What personal cleaning have you done for yourself? What prompted you to act?
- Sometimes personal cleaning comes as a surprise. It can happen when something difficult challenges us or something sad moves us or something awesome inspires us. Has that ever happened to you?

For Children

When Jesus talks to people, they listen to him and want to hear what he has to say.
- Who is someone you like to listen to?
- Who is someone who reads you stories or tells you stories?

A person with an unclean spirit comes to Jesus, and Jesus makes the person clean.
- Did you ever fall in some mud and get really dirty? How hard was it to get clean?
- Did you ever help an adult clean a dirty car or a dirty room?
- What was the dirtiest thing you ever had to clean? How long did it take? Did you get any help? What was it like?

Closing

Example is not the main thing in life—it is the only thing. —Albert Schweitzer

(Mission 2000: B Cycle)

Fifth Sunday of the Year

6 February 2000
9 February 2003
5 February 2006

Getting Well

Scripture

- *Job 7:1–4,6–7.* Job's unhappy comments demonstrate for us that there are times when we feel miserable, and those situations and emotions are very real for us.
- *1 Corinthians 9:16–19,22–23.* Paul describes his compulsion to preach, his desire to do so freely without any payment or recompense, and his style of being all things to all people so the Gospel message is shared.
- *Mark 1:29–39.* Jesus cures Simon's mother-in-law, as well as others. After prayer, he presses his followers to move on to other towns so that he might continue preaching the Good News of salvation.

Theme

Job, Paul, and Jesus all speak of their daily work experiences and what they are called to do. Job is unhappy because of all his suffering, and he sees his days as drudgery. Paul is almost a workaholic, focused on doing whatever it takes to spread the Gospel. Jesus cures the fever of Simon's mother-in-law, and her immediate response is to get up and serve them. Jesus escapes all the crowds early the next morning by finding a lonely place to pray, and from there he urges his followers to press on with him to other villages and continue their work.

Focusing Object
A thermometer

Reflections

For Adults

Jesus is clear about what his work needs to be. Curing is important. Spreading the Good News of salvation is just as important. Getting rid of demons is important.

- What do you see as your main "work"?
- Have you ever thought of writing a personal mission statement? If so, what kinds of things would it involve?
- As soon as Simon's mother-in-law is cured of her fever, she gets up and begins to wait on Jesus, Simon, Andrew, James, and John. What do you suppose this unnamed woman saw as her personal call to work?

Jesus obviously saw prayer as a priority in his life. Often the Gospel stories find him escaping the crowds to be alone and pray. It seems to be the place where he gathers his strength and finds his focus.

- Is prayer a priority in your life? How so?
- Is prayer a place where you find strength and focus? Is prayer a place where you celebrate the strength and focus you've already found elsewhere? Is prayer itself a place you still search for? What is prayer like for you?
- It's hard to cooperate with evil when you lead a life of prayer. How might prayer affect the rest of your day? How might prayer affect your life's work?

For Teenagers

In this Gospel story, Jesus sees his work as involving three areas: curing, teaching, and praying.

- Not only did Jesus cure the fever of Simon's mother-in-law but he cured many other ill people who came looking for him at her door. Obviously we can't cure sicknesses as Jesus did, but we can be a healing presence for someone going through a difficult time or a personal struggle. When and how have you done that for someone?

- Jesus wanted to travel to other villages to preach and teach. Are you a good student? Are you willing to listen and learn? Do you want to become more educated? How so? Obviously you can't be a certified teacher yet, but you can teach others by the example of your life. What can others learn from you by watching the way you live?
- Jesus escaped the crowds to pray. Do you ever need quiet time, away from noise and activity, so that you can make sense of the world? If so, how does that time help you? If not, how might that kind of time help you?

For Children

Simon's mother-in-law is sick with a high fever. As soon as Jesus arrives, they tell him about her fever. Jesus takes her hand, and her fever goes away.

- Have you ever had a fever? How does it feel to have a fever?
- What made your fever finally go away? How did you feel then?

So many people come to see Jesus because they want to be cured. But he still finds time to pray and to be alone with God, because praying is so important.

- What prayers do you know?
- Do you ever pray in your own words? What is it like when you pray in your own way?

Closing

Now I get me up to work,
I pray the Lord I may not shirk,
And if I die before tonight,
I pray my work will be all right.
　　　　　　—Thomas Osborne Davis

(Mission 2000: B Cycle)

Sixth Sunday of the Year

13 February 2000
16 February 2003
12 February 2006

Reclaiming the Outcast

Scripture

- ○ *Leviticus 13:1–2,44–46.* The Jewish regulations regarding leprosy are stated—how the condition must be officially identified, how the priest must declare the person unclean, and what the person with the disease must do.
- • *1 Corinthians 10:31—11:1.* Paul is reminding us that strict dietary laws governing what we eat and drink are not as important as how we live and how we treat others. We must not offend others but be sensitive to all persons. In essence we must imitate Jesus.
- ○ *Mark 1:40–45.* Jesus cures the person with leprosy, and the miracle is so great, the newly healed one cannot keep it a secret.

Theme

In Leviticus strict religious laws are stated; the unclean are to be separated and not touched by others. In Corinthians religious laws are put into perspective: living as Jesus lived is more important than the specifics of our diet. But Jesus goes the distance in the Gospel. He doesn't merely tell us that the old laws that are strict, disrespectful, and unnecessary are less important than our human interactions and the needs of others. He steps over the line by actually breaking the laws and bringing healing in the process. He touches the untouchable, and suddenly the one he touches is no longer untouchable.

Focusing Object
A piece of torn cloth

Reflections

For Adults

According to the old Law, the lepers have to tear their garments, shave their heads, live in a designated unclean area, and shout "Unclean" as they walk about, to warn others to stay away. Their self-respect is stripped from them; they are scorned by all of society at the time they most need love, care, and support.

- Besides persons with other contagious diseases, who does our society scorn and strip of their dignity? Who especially needs the love, care, and support that we do not always give?

Mark's Gospel contains an element Scripture scholars call the "Messianic Secret." Jesus is often depicted telling others not to reveal what they know of his power. Jesus tells this newly cured person to return to the priest.

Persons suspected of leprosy are to be confined, then to return in seven days so the priest can re-examine the sores and proclaim the person to be clean or unclean, depending on whether the sore has healed or not. A purification rite is outlined in Leviticus for priests to use with persons who have leprosy. Jesus evidently doesn't want this person's cure to be linked with his divine powers, but the person who is cured can't keep it a secret; he tells everyone.

- What were some short-term and long-term consequences (for Jesus) of this cured person telling the secret?

For Teenagers

Jesus tells this person that he cures to keep it a secret and merely go back to the priest, but this person tells everyone about Jesus.

- Do you think Jesus was angry with him for not keeping the secret?
- Why do you think he disobeyed Jesus?

Once Jesus' reputation spreads, many things happen. He often is followed by mobs of people, and he isn't able to get away and rest. He is often pursued not because of his preaching and his message but for his ability to cure and perform miracles. Because so many people believe in him, his influence grows, and the political and religious rulers are jealous and afraid of the power he is gaining.

- What do you think the Apostles thought of all this? If you had walked the roads with Jesus, what would you think of his powers and his knowledge?
- Would the large groups of people bother and inconvenience you? Would you feel popular and powerful as well? Would you be concerned with the political or religious leaders and their jealousy? Would you want to stay with Jesus or leave him? Why?

For Children

A very sick person comes up to Jesus. He doesn't tell Jesus he wants to be cured. Instead he tells Jesus that he believes in him. He tells Jesus, "I know you can make me better if you want to." And Jesus tells the person, "I want to." With one touch that person is cured. He isn't sick anymore.

- What if the person wasn't so nice to Jesus? What if the person was nasty or demanded to be cured? Do you think Jesus still would have made him better? Why or why not?

After he cures this sick person, Jesus tells him not to tell anyone. But this person is too excited to keep it a secret. He is so happy about his good news that he tells everyone.

- If Jesus came to you and did something wonderful, but then told you to keep it a secret, what would you do? Would it be easy or hard to keep that secret?

Closing

As soon as healing takes place, go out and heal somebody else. —Maya Angelou

(Acts of Faith)

Seventh Sunday of the Year

Ways to
Get in Touch
with Jesus

Scripture

- *Isaiah 43:18–19,21–22,24–25.* Isaiah foretells a new way of doing things and asks for openness. God is the one who completely forgives sins.
- *2 Corinthians 1:18–22.* Paul tells us that our faith must be complete. It cannot go back and forth. We must say amen and believe.
- *Mark 2:1–12.* Jesus forgives sins and cures a person who is paralyzed, a person who is lowered into the crowded room through the roof.

Theme

Jesus is completely new. He does things that have never been done before. We can't be saying yes to him sometimes and no to him other times. We must commit and believe and follow completely. We must have the tenacity of the four people who so badly wanted their friend to be healed that they climbed on top of the roof, cut out a hole, and lowered the person in from above. They couldn't figure out how to get into the room the conventional way, so they tried something new.

Focusing Object
A rope

Reflections

For Adults

This picture is almost humorous. The four friends of the person who is paralyzed have absolutely no doubts regarding Jesus' power. Yet the very religious scribes have nothing but doubt. They are quite upset when Jesus forgives the sins of the person lowered into the room from the roof. Then they are amazed when they see that Jesus can perform a miracle cure.

- Which is the most important and most dramatic act of healing that Jesus performs: the forgiving of sins or the curing of paralysis? Which gets the most positive attention? Which gets negative attention? What does all this say about Jesus' mission and our readiness to accept why he came to us?
- Whose faith is yours most like: that of the four friends who would try anything to get an audience with Jesus for their friend, that of the scribes who sat back and criticized, or that of the general crowd who packed the house to listen to what Jesus had to say and to see who this famous person was?

For Teenagers

Imagine that you are in a crowded place—a mall, a concert, an athletic event. Imagine that you really want to get inside to see one important person, but there is no room at the door, and the number of people is tremendous.

- Would you ever consider climbing on the roof and cutting a hole through it? Why or why not? What modern consequences might you have to deal with that weren't around in the days of Jesus?

Modern circumstances aside, it was quite an original idea for these four people to lower their friend to Jesus through the roof. It was a very unusual solution to their problem of having to find a way in.

- Have you ever found an unusual solution to a difficult problem? What was the problem? What was your solution? How did it work?

For Children

There was a person who couldn't walk or move too much, because of an awful sickness. Four people really believe that Jesus can make their friend's sickness go away. But when they try to bring their friend to Jesus, it is just too crowded. They can't get through the door. They can't get into the room where Jesus is.

- If you were the person who was being carried on a blanket or a cot or a hammock, and your friends told you about their plan to climb up on the roof, cut a hole in it, and lower you through the ceiling with ropes, what would you say? Would you be afraid they might drop you? Would you be afraid that Jesus might be angry with you? Would you think that their idea wouldn't work?
- If you were the person who owned the house, would you be angry that four people you didn't know climbed onto your roof and cut a hole it? Would you feel sorry for the person who was sick and wanted to see Jesus, or would you chase all those people out of your house? Why? Would you ask them to help you fix the roof when they were finished?
- What do you think Jesus would say to you?

Closing

You're either a part of the solution or a part of the problem. —Eldridge Cleaver

(Vision 2000: A Cycle)

Eighth Sunday of the Year

27 February 2000
2 March 2003
26 February 2006

Old and New

Scripture

- *Hosea 2:16–17,21–22.* As a holy man, Hosea's marriage to Gomer (a prostitute) is compared to God's love for the chosen people (who have been unfaithful). These words demonstrate to us the covenant of God's love, even when we do not deserve that love.
- *2 Corinthians 3:1–6.* Paul tries to describe his confidence in God by comparing the written to the unwritten. He needs no written proof of God. Written laws can be misinterpreted and can bring harm; the law of the Spirit brings life.
- *Mark 2:18–22.* Jesus teaches us to be aware of the old and the new. New patches sown on old clothes will tear away; new wine will break old wineskins.

Theme

The old way is to get written proof and to follow exactly the letter of the law—to have a contract that clearly spells out the terms. The new way is simply to trust and commit. The spirit of the law is more important than the letter of the law. The promise of unconditional love is better than a written letter of recommendation. Jesus tells us it's time to stop fasting and time to start celebrating that he is here with us, that God is here with us in our own human flesh. The old is gone, and we need to be ready for the new.

Focusing Object
A patch of cloth

Reflections

For Adults

Jesus is asked a simple question: "Why do you not do things the way others do them, the way they have always been done?" Jesus has a good answer: "When things change, we must do things in a different way."
- When have you been in a new situation and discovered that old strategies aren't working? How did you change your approach?

Jesus' new way of not fasting and not always following the Jewish laws with precise accuracy is very troubling to the more established, deeply religious people of his day.
- What traditions have you enjoyed in the past, but watched with pain as they faded away? How did you adjust to their absence?
- What new traditions had you resisted at first but finally came to accept and appreciate? How did you adjust to them?

For Teenagers

Jesus' situation is very familiar to teenagers. Young people are used to trying things in new and different ways, and the older generations often question why things have to change: "What's wrong with the way we've always done things?"
- When have you been in a situation where you tried something new, and people who weren't used to it questioned you about why you were doing things in a new way? How did you respond? What did you say to justify your new, improved way of doing things? Was your explanation accepted? Why or why not?

Change can be very complicated. Very often, as time goes by, people learn new and better ways to do things, and people who don't like change find it difficult to adjust. But all old ways are not bad simply because they are old. Many changes are an improvement over the past. But some changes are for the worse, not for the better.

At the beginning of the twentieth century, women couldn't vote. Today, women can vote, they can become experts in any field they wish, and they are treated with equality and greater respect than in the past. This is an example of a good change.

- What are other changes you think are improvements from the past? How are things better than they used to be?

At the beginning of the twentieth century, it was commonplace to leave your doors unlocked. Neighbors knew one another's names and families, and some of their daily routines. Violence was very rare, and children could play outside into the darkness without fear of being kidnapped, robbed, mugged, or hurt in any way. Today there are drive-by shootings and letter bombs and random acts of violence that make our world a more frightening place. This is an example of a bad change.

- What are other changes you can think of that are not improvements from the past? How are things worse than they used to be? How did they become this way, and what can be done to improve conditions?

For Children

Jesus was a person who tried some new things and did some old things in a different way. Other people didn't always understand him or what he was trying to do. Sometimes new things don't always blend well with old things.

- Jesus warned the people not to sew new, unshrunk patches on old cloth, or the patch will shrink and pull away from the old cloth to make a bigger hole. Have you ever sewn anything? a button? a sock puppet? a sewing card? How does sewing work? What do you do with the yarn or thread?

- Jesus warned the people not to pour new wine into old wineskins, or they would break. We don't use wineskins anymore, but we can still break something old by putting something new into it. What would happen if you bought a new bigger, fluffier pillow and tried to squeeze it into an old, shrunken pillowcase?

Closing

If you always do what you always did, you will always get what you always got. —Jackie "Moms" Mabley

(Acts of Faith)

Ninth Sunday of the Year

5 March 2000

*The readings
for this Sunday
do not occur
in 2003 or 2006.*

Healing
and Healed

Scripture

- *Deuteronomy 5:12–15.* The third commandment tells us that God, whose mighty hand saved the chosen people from slavery in Egypt, commands us to remember to keep holy the Sabbath day, and to not work.
- *2 Corinthians 4:6–11.* Paul reminds us that we are heavenly treasure in earthen vessels, that inside our mortal bodies that will die, we have an eternal soul that will live forever.
- *Mark 2:23—3:6* Jesus does some unlawful things on the Sabbath: he and his followers pluck grain from the fields, and he heals the withered hand of a person in the synagogue. Shortly afterward the Pharisees and Herodians begin to plot how they might get rid of Jesus.

Theme

Once again the people watching Jesus must deal with the way Jesus does things in a new and different way. It is very troubling for the pious, conservative religious watching Jesus to try and understand why he would break the laws of the Sabbath. God commands all people to rest on the Sabbath, so no work should be done. Jesus gives an example of when even David broke a religious law, showing the people how the spirit of the law is more important than the letter of the law. Jesus also heals a person in the synagogue, but that only makes the Pharisees more upset, and they plot against him. Paul tells us that we too, as followers of Jesus, will suffer persecution, but that we will rise in the end as well.

Focusing Object
A glove, or a cutout of a hand

Reflections

For Adults

Jesus gets in trouble because he isn't someone who always plays the game by the establishment's rules. If the rules don't serve a purpose, or if they get in the way of God's work, then Jesus will bend them a bit. Both the political and the religious authorities feel threatened by his power and influence, and they know they have to destroy him.

- When have you seen a gifted, talented person do good things and then get "destroyed" because someone in power feels jealous or afraid of this person's ability? What happened? What was your response when it happened? What could have stopped it?
- Have you bent the rules when you found they didn't serve their purpose, or when they got in the way? How do you know when you're bending the rules because of your own laziness or selfishness, or when you're doing it for a noble and righteous reason?

Paul warns us that if we follow Jesus, the same things will happen to us. We will be persecuted when we challenge others, yet we will eventually rise.

- When have you challenged the status quo because it went against the way Jesus would have things? What have been the unpleasant consequences? How did you handle them?
- How do you see yourself acting in future similar situations? Will you become more bold, or will you be more subtle? Why?

Often we hear about people in the Gospels whose life is never the same after Jesus' healing touch, but we have no details because they are minor characters of little importance.

- This person with the withered hand is in the synagogue already. We don't know if it is common knowledge that Jesus is going there. Perhaps he is expected there, so many people who need healing have gathered there with the hope of a cure. Perhaps Jesus is not expected, and the only people at the synagogue are there to pray. Either way, what do you suppose it was like for this person to be healed and suddenly to have two healthy hands?
- If you had a withered hand that was suddenly healed, and you knew the holy person who cured you was in political and religious trouble, do you think you would stay with him anyway and suffer the consequences bravely? Or do you think you would want to just get away, eager to live a normal life for the first time? Why?

Jesus broke the Sabbath by having his followers pick grain in the fields, and later by healing on the Sabbath.

- Do you think that is the main reason that the Pharisees (religious leaders) and the Herodians (government and political leaders) were so upset with Jesus? What else do you think was going on? Why else would they be so upset with what was happening with Jesus?

For Children

Jesus helps someone on the Sabbath: a person whose hand is withered and weak. Jesus heals the withered hand and makes it strong. Some people think Jesus shouldn't have done that, because it is a little like working, and working isn't allowed on the Sabbath day. Jesus also picks some grain in the fields to eat. That is like working, too.

- If you were there with the people who were angry about what Jesus did, what would you say?

Do you think Jesus should be criticized for doing what he did? Why or why not?

- If you were the person who had a withered hand, and Jesus cured it and made it strong and well again, what would you say? What would you do? What would you tell people about Jesus? What would you say about the people who were angry and thought Jesus shouldn't have done it?
- What are some things that you do with your hands? What are some things that you can do with only one hand? What are some things you need two hands to do?

Closing

With your hands you make your success, with your hands you destroy success. —A Yoruba proverb

(Acts of Faith)

Tenth Sunday of the Year

The readings for this Sunday do not occur in 2000, 2003, or 2006.

Jesus' Family

Scripture

- *Genesis 3:9–15.* After Adam and Eve's sin is discovered, God explains the future hardships due to the snake's trickery.
- *2 Corinthians 4:13—5:1.* Jesus was raised, so we will be raised. Any earthly pain we see and experience is only temporary; our future glory, which we cannot see yet, will be eternal. This earthly house may crumble, but our heavenly house will last forever.
- *Mark 3:20–35.* If a house is divided against itself, that family will not be able to endure. Those who do God's will are the sisters and brothers and family of Jesus.

Theme

Our ancestors explained the pains and struggles of life with the story of Adam and Eve's sin; humanity's first sin was punished with the hardships we all must endure now. Paul comforts us by reminding us that our earthly home and hardships are only temporary; the glory of heaven is a house that will last eternally. Jesus teaches us that if a nation or a family stays strong together, it will not fall. This strength comes from the Holy Spirit, and sins against the Spirit are the hardest to forgive. Those who follow the Spirit, stay strong together, and do God's will are the ones whom Jesus calls his brothers and sisters.

Focusing Object
A family picture, or some representation of a family

Reflections

For Adults

The Holy Spirit is what works within our soul and encourages us to stay strong, to follow the will of God, and to resist the evil temptations that may lure us away from what is right. As long as we are open to the promptings of the Holy Spirit, we can recognize and resist when we are being motivated by things such as power, money, prestige, control, or fear. Once we turn off our connection to the Spirit, we stop listening to our conscience, and we stop caring about what is right or wrong.

- Have you ever gotten to the point of resisting the Spirit? Have you ever come close to letting the promise of power, money, prestige, or control speak louder than your own conscience? Have you ever been more motivated by fear than by love?

A nation or a family divided against itself cannot stand. Yet hardship happens.

- In what ways is our nation divided? What are the main issues causing the division? What can responsible citizens do to help build up the strength of the nation?
- In what ways has your own family been divided? How have you been able to nourish yourselves and bring back health?

For Teenagers

Very small children do things without considering the consequences. They aren't old enough to have a developed conscience to help them sort out right and wrong. But as we become older, we develop our ability to distinguish between a sinful choice and a good choice. If we stop listening to our conscience, we will lose that connection to the Holy Spirit that guides us.

- Think back to when you were a child, beginning to develop your conscience. When was a time you were aware of a sinful act you committed, and you hesitated to make things right as you considered what you had done?
- When was a more recent time that you worked to make things right after a poor choice?
- Have you ever felt the "pangs of guilt" after doing something wrong, yet tried your best to ignore them? What happened?

  A house and a family that are strong will stand and endure.

- What are the strengths of your house and your family? What are the weaknesses?
- When there is a weakness, how does your family address it? What kinds of conversations take place in your family to make things right again?
- When is a time that you needed extra help or it took extra effort to stay healthy as a family and home?

For Children

This Gospel story tells us that everyone who does what God wants is a brother or a sister of Jesus.
- When do you do what God wants?
- What do you think it means to be Jesus' brother or sister?
- If Jesus came to live in your house for a week as a special visitor who could play with you and talk with you and eat meals with you, what kinds of things do you think Jesus would want to do with you? What kinds of things would you want to do with Jesus?
- Do you share a room with a brother or a sister? If you do, what is it like? If you don't, would you like to?
- If Jesus was your real human brother or sister, who always lived at your house, would you want to share a room with Jesus? Why or why not?

Closing

Life is fragile—handle with prayer. —E. C. McKenzie

(Action 2000: C Cycle)

Eleventh Sunday of the Year

The readings for this Sunday do not occur in 2000, 2003, or 2006.

From the Tiniest Seed

Scripture

- *Ezekiel 17:22–24.* This poetry proclaims Yahweh as the careful God who will make the green tree wither and cause the withered tree to become green again, who will bring honor and dignity back to Judah and to all people who have been oppressed.
- *2 Corinthians 5:6–10.* Paul reminds us that we walk by faith and not by sight, that we can be confident about what comes with our future heavenly reward, based on how faithfully we live out our life on earth.
- *Mark 4:26–34.* Jesus compares the Reign of God to the way seeds grow, and especially to the way the mustard seed grows.

Theme

Seeds are such tiny and unassuming things—who would imagine the power and force they can release as they grow and become something huge and magnificent. How it happens is a mystery—even to the farmers who plant them and nurture them. They sow by faith, not by sight, believing that somehow the miracle will happen again and they will have a crop. Ezekiel tells us how Yahweh will bring new life to the lifeless and will wither the life that is growing badly. Jesus tells us that the Reign of God is as mysterious as the seed that grows, and as surprisingly powerful as the tiniest seed that becomes the biggest shrub.

Focusing Object
A seed

Reflections

For Adults

Jesus tells us how mysterious the Reign of God is—like a tiny seed that mysteriously grows into a huge bush. The farmer can't truly take responsibility for its growth, even if it was well nourished. It's a miracle that just happens in an astonishing way. And it happens so regularly that we come to depend upon it and expect seeds to grow. We trust that if we sow the seeds, the growth will happen, even though we don't understand how.

- What seeds do you sow? Do you always trust that they will grow? Why or why not?
- Who has been able to affect your life by sowing seeds for you?

Jesus' three years of ministry with a dozen or so committed followers is a tiny seed that leads to the explosion of Christianity. It is a way of life that "sells itself." People don't have to hear long explanations or sales pitches; they see the way the Christians live, they see the peace in their hearts and the conviction of their faith, and they want to be part of that vibrant community. Jesus' followers are living the Good News, not only preaching it. And good news gets around.

- Is the Christian way of life as strong a living example today as it was in the early church? Can people recognize those who are "Christian" (or who claim to be) by the way they live? Why or why not?
- When are you a living Gospel? What are some ways that you live the Good News of Christianity? How does your good news sell itself?

For Teenagers

Jesus tells us that a tiny seed can blossom into a huge growth.

- What is a tiny interest or hobby you may have started a long time ago as a "seed" that has now grown into a big, important part of your life?
- Who is a person that started out as just an acquaintance of yours but whose relationship with you has now grown into an important and very close friendship?

In the early church, the Christians are recognized right away as honest, selfless, generous, loving, forgiving people. People can tell they are Christians just by the way they live, and it is so inspiring that people want to join their faith community and be just like them. Christians didn't have to carry signs or wear T-shirts to advertise themselves; people just knew how wonderful they were.

- Is it easy to tell who's a Christian today? Can you observe someone's behavior and know whether they are a follower of Jesus? Why or why not?
- Some very violent behavior is happening in the world today in the name of God and religion. Can you think of any examples? Some very helpful, peaceful behavior is also happening today that has nothing to do with formal religion. Can you think of any examples? How do these trends affect the way many young people view religion? How do these trends affect the way you yourself view the church?

For Children

Jesus teaches us that a very tiny seed like the mustard seed can grow into the biggest shrub.

- Have you ever planted a seed? What did it grow into?
- Where is the biggest bush or tree you have ever seen? What do you think it grew from?
- Have you ever tasted mustard? Do you like it? If so, what do you put it on?

Every big, grown-up person started out as a tiny baby.

- How are babies and grown-ups like seeds and trees?
- How big do you think you will grow to be?

Closing

A good thing sells itself. A bad thing is advertised.
—A Swahili proverb
(Native Wisdom for White Minds)

Twelfth Sunday of the Year

The readings for this Sunday do not occur in 2000 or 2003.

25 June 2006

Jesus Calms the Wind and the Sea

Scripture

- *Job 38:1,8–11.* When Job questions the logic or the justice in his own situation, Yahweh answers by questioning Job with some mighty matters he cannot answer. We can never hope to understand the enormity of God's ways, but we must trust that things somehow will work out, and that blessings can eventually come from suffering.
- *2 Corinthians 5:14–17.* Jesus died for us so that we might truly live. Jesus' Resurrection is our resurrection, too. We are all new creations due to Jesus' love.
- *Mark 4:35–41.* Jesus sleeps in a boat as a storm kicks up, and the frightened disciples wake up Jesus. He criticizes their lack of faith, and then calms the wind and the waves.

Theme

Mark's entire Gospel emphasizes the Messianic Secret, and this story is a good example of that emphasis. The disciples watch the almighty power at Jesus' hands, and they ask one another: "Who is this man? What is this all about?" Jesus doesn't give them a satisfying answer, although he asks them why their faith is so weak. So they are left to wonder. Like the disciples and like Job, we too are confused by Yahweh's vast and mighty plan; it is too much for our human and limited minds. But we can understand Paul's simple message: Jesus' deep love gives us new life.

Focusing Object
A boat or ship

Reflections

For Adults

In Mark's Gospel, people are often confused about the powers and identity of Jesus. He is quite a mystery. As the Apostles witness him in action, they can't help but ask, "Who is this man?" In this way Mark's Gospel emphasizes the process of faith, the steps we go through in our faith journey that eventually lead to committed faith.

- What are some steps you have had to take in your faith journey? How did you arrive at the place where you are now in regard to your relationship with God?
- When has your faith been very weak? How did it become strong again?
- When have you clearly felt God's presence and support?

In our everyday life, we don't witness miracles as directly as the Apostles did—we don't see Jesus calming the sea and wind or easing the traffic when we long for a more peaceful drive home.

- Do you still believe in miracles? Why or why not?
- Have you ever sensed a time when you believe Jesus had a direct hand in some event in your life?
- How would you explain to a non-Christian your answer to the question, "Who is Jesus?"

For Teenagers

Jesus calms the storm when the disciples wake him up.

- Have you ever been in a boat or ship during a storm? If so, what was it like?
- How would you react if you were in a storm in the middle of a lake with some of your friends, and one of them just stood up and told the wind

and waves to stop? *And they did stop!* How would you feel? Petrified? Shocked? Courageous? Would you be afraid of this person's powers? Would you think that they might be evil? Would you think that they might be saintly? What would you say?

Many times we feel as if our life is stormy. Like the disciples, we might feel as if our boat is about to crash. But Jesus doesn't help them until they ask him to. They don't see the difference he can make until they initiate contact with him and ask for his help.

- When your life is stormy, do you ride it out alone or do you ask Jesus for help? Explain.
- What does it actually mean to ask Jesus for help? What expectations do you have for that request? What do you think Jesus does for a person who asks for help? How can asking Jesus really help anything?

For Children

Jesus is in a boat with his friends, but he is sleeping. When a terrible storm starts up, his friends become afraid and they wake up Jesus.

- Why do you think they woke up Jesus? Why didn't they just let him sleep if he was tired?
- How do you think his friends felt? Do you think they were feeling brave or afraid?

Once his friends wake him, Jesus yells at the wind and the water for being so rough and wild. He tells the weather to calm down and become gentle again. And it does!

- If you were in that boat with Jesus' friends, how would you feel?
- Would you be surprised at what Jesus could do?
- Have you ever been on a boat or a ship? If you have been, what was it like? If you haven't been on a boat or a ship, do you think you might like to go on one? Why or why not?

Closing

A ship in port is safe, but that's not what ships are built for. —Grace Murray Hopper

(Success Every Day)

Thirteenth Sunday of the Year

2 July 2000
29 June 2003
2 July 2006

Daring to
Touch Jesus

Scripture

- *Wisdom 1:13–15; 2:23–24.* Our God is a God of living, and all God's creations are formed that they might live and be.
- *2 Corinthians 8:7,9,13–15.* When we are blessed, we are to give to those who are in need; when we are in need, we will be blessed by the generosity of those who share with us.
- *Mark 5:21–43.* On his way to see Jairus's daughter, Jesus is interrupted by a woman with a disease, who brings on her own cure by touching the hem of Jesus' robe.

Theme

The Book of Wisdom proclaims that our God is a God of living; Paul reminds us that our call is to be generous to those who suffer. In Mark's Gospel Jesus demonstrates both principles. He raises a little girl from the dead and he praises a woman for being brave and faithful enough to reach out and grab for the garment she believes will cure her.

Focusing Object
A bathrobe

Reflections

For Adults

Jesus' ministry is the ministry of interruption. It is not the ministry of time wasters but the ministry of unexpected, important matters that hurting people bring to him. On the way to give care to Jairus's daughter, a woman reaches out to touch Jesus' robe, and he feels the power of healing take place. He could have ignored it; after all, he is on his way to see someone who is deathly ill, and every minute counts. But he takes the time to stop and discover what has happened. Perhaps Jairus is thinking that such an interruption might cost him his little girl's life. But Jesus doesn't let that happen.

- How is your life a series of interruptions? How do you deal with interruptions?
- Which of your interruptions are simply time wasters and matters of no importance? Which of your interruptions are actually matters that are more important than whatever work you were originally involved in?
- How does a person learn to distinguish between the time-wasting interruptions and the life-saving ones?

The Messianic Secret of Mark's Gospel is illustrated in this passage. Jesus doesn't seem to want people to be aware of who he is too quickly. Faith is a process that progresses gradually. So Mark portrays Jesus as being completely in control, and the followers as not understanding him. Even when he raises the little girl from the dead, he tells the people not to let anyone know what has happened.

- Jesus seems to say the strangest things. In a crowd full of people bumping into one another, he asks, "Who touched me?" When he comes upon a home of grief-stricken family members, he asks them why they are all wailing. In what way does Jesus' message in our modern world still seem strange?

- An astonishing truth, such as the Messianic Secret, is hard to take all at once. Sometimes we are told things in stages, so we are better prepared to accept the reality of a situation. When has this happened to you?

For Teenagers

This woman who struggles to touch Jesus' robe is in a desperate situation. The Gospel tells us that she has been bleeding for twelve years. That's hard to imagine. In those days any woman who was bleeding was seen as unclean until her period of bleeding was over. So not only does she touch Jesus' robe and receive power without asking for it (she steals something that belongs to someone else), but she is out in public, mingling with other people, while she is in fact unclean (and thus causing all of them to risk being made unclean). She should have been reprimanded, but Jesus praises her.

- What does Jesus' praise of this woman say about his view of the cultural practice of keeping the "unclean" women away from other "clean" people?
- Besides curing this woman's medical condition, how else does Jesus heal her and restore her dignity?
- As men in a society that views women as people who become unclean every month, Jesus' disciples must have had a hard time with this. What do you suppose they were thinking, and how do you think Jesus' actions challenged their attitudes toward women?

When Jesus goes in to see Jairus's daughter, he lets only Peter, James, and John go in with him. The rest of the followers have to stay outside. Jesus did this a lot; Peter, James, and John get to do lots of things that the others aren't invited to do.

- How do you think the other disciples reacted to this?
- Why do you think Jesus would behave in such a way—having favorites?

- Do you think Peter, James, and John kept it a secret from the other Apostles that Jesus had raised the little girl from the dead, or do you think they told the others? Do you think the young girl's family members kept it a secret, or do you think they told people about it? Why?

For Children

In this Gospel story, Jesus takes care of two people—a woman who had been sick for twelve years and a little girl who is so sick, she actually dies.
- How do you think Jesus wants us to treat people who are sick?
- When have you been sick? How did your family treat you? What was done to take care of you?
- Have you ever helped take care of someone who was sick? What did you do?

Closing

The honor of one is the honor of all. The hurt of one is the hurt of all. —Phil Lane Jr., Yankton Sioux/Chickasaw

(Native Wisdom for White Minds)

Fourteenth Sunday of the Year

9 July 2000
6 July 2003
9 July 2006

𝔍esus, the
Carpenter
Prophet

Scripture

- *Ezekiel 2:2–5.* Ezekiel is warned by the Holy Spirit that although he is a prophet, many will rebel and will not want to listen to him.
- *2 Corinthians 12:7–10.* Paul tells of his physical ailment, and of his prayer to be relieved; Jesus's reply to him in prayer makes him realize that power can come from weakness, and that the grace of Jesus is all he needs.
- *Mark 6:1–6.* Jesus returns to his hometown, and his old neighbors reject him. They can't imagine that the Jesus they remember, the carpenter's son, could have grown up to become a preacher and prophet.

Theme

Like Ezekiel, Jesus is rejected by people too rebellious to listen. Like Paul, Jesus finds that there is power in weakness nonetheless, and he sets out to preach in the towns where people are more open to what he has to say.

Focusing Object
A tool box, or individual tools

Reflections

For Adults

Jesus is rejected by his former neighbors, the people he knew by name, the people who watched him as he grew up and observed him in his different stages of development. Perhaps they saw him giggle with the neighborhood kids; perhaps they saw him cut his fingers in his father's carpenter shop as he learned the trade. Perhaps they heard the story about when he was twelve years old and was missing for three days, and his parents had to go back to Jerusalem to search for him. Perhaps they helped them search. Perhaps they wondered why he left town.

- In what ways is their attitude toward Jesus understandable and reasonable?
- In what ways is their attitude toward Jesus tragic or unreasonable?

Jesus, the divine Son of God, the Messiah and Savior of the world, is unable to work miracles in his own hometown because he is so distressed by the lack of faith the townspeople have in his abilities.

- What does this inability tell us about Jesus as a person?
- What does this story tell us about the role of affirmation and support in our own family and circle of friends?
- What does this story call you to be more aware of in the future?

For Teenagers

When Jesus comes back home, his neighbors remember Jesus the kid, and refuse to believe in the talents and gifts of Jesus the adult and prophet.

- How would it be if you grew up, became famous at your craft or skill, and returned home to discover that everyone who knew you as a child had a hard time respecting you as an accomplished expert in your field? What would you do? How would you react?
- How would it be if one of your friends who never seemed particularly gifted in any one area grew up, left town, and became famous for her or

his talent and insight and opinions? How would you respond to her or his sudden popularity? How might you feel about this friend?

When Jesus returns to visit his hometown, people are not very supportive. They just have a hard time accepting that the child they knew is now a famous prophet, healer, and speaker. Jesus is so distressed by their lack of confidence in his ability and their lack of trust that he cannot even perform the miracles he wants to.

- Why not? What do you think?
- How does the support of your friends and family affect your own performance level and ability?

For Children

When Jesus comes back home to his old neighborhood, his family members and old friends don't believe he is anyone special. This makes Jesus feel very sad.

- Do your friends and family think you are special? How do you know?
- How would you feel if they stopped liking you and caring about you?
- What would you have said if you were there with Jesus' old friends? What if they tried to tell you that Jesus wasn't really that smart? What if they tried to tell you that he couldn't really do any miracles? What would you say to them?
- What would you say to Jesus to help him feel better?

Closing

To the preacher who kept saying, "We must put God in our lives," the Master said, "God is already there. Our business is to recognize this."
—Anthony de Mello

(Vision 2000: A Cycle)

Fifteenth Sunday of the Year

16 July 2000
13 July 2003
16 July 2006

Sent Forth
As Apostles

Scripture

- *Amos 7:12–15.* Amaziah tells Amos to go do his prophetic work someplace else.
- *Ephesians 1:3–14.* Jesus has redeemed us and our sins are forgiven. We are chosen, and when we hear the word of God and believe, we receive the Holy Spirit.
- *Mark 6:7–13.* Jesus commissions the Twelve to go out, two by two, as missionaries, with no extra clothes, no food, and no money—just a walking stick. Their task? To proclaim the Good News to whoever will hear it. If they find listeners, they are to stay. And if they do not? They are to leave, shaking the dust from their feet.

Theme

This is not easy work we have. We hear the word of God, we believe, and we receive the Holy Spirit. Now the hard part begins. Like Amos, we will be told sometimes to take our religion elsewhere. Like the Twelve, we have no plan and no idea of the future. When we find someone who wants to share our faith, we are to stick around. If not, we are to shake the dust and move on.

Focusing Object

A walking stick

Reflections

Jesus tells us some concrete things about our mission in life: Go in pairs; it's not good to go alone. Stay where you are welcomed. Don't force yourself on someone unwilling to listen. Take a walking stick, or whatever you need to help support you on the journey.

- When have you felt alone on your journey? When have you felt partnered?
- When have you journeyed and found a welcome?
- When have you had to "shake the dust from your feet and move on"?
- Besides people, what supports you in your journey? What's your personal walking stick?

Jesus asks the Twelve to go forth with a mission, but with no map, no agenda, no plan, and no provisions. They basically have to go forth on faith alone. They take the risk.

- When do you feel as if you are journeying with nothing but faith?
- Is faith always enough? Why or why not?
- Do you see yourself as a risk taker? Why or why not?

Jesus obviously has faith in the Apostles to give them this challenge. He believes in them.

- Do you think Jesus believes in you? Do you believe in yourself?

Jesus tells the Twelve to go out in pairs, so friendship must be important. Jesus doesn't want us to go it alone.

- Who are your closest friends?
- What do you like about your friends? What do they like about you?

Jesus tells the Twelve to stay where they are welcome, and to leave when they are not.

- Where do you feel welcome? Where is a place you feel safe and secure? Why is that?
- When have you not felt welcome? When have you had to just move on because things were not working out the way you had hoped.

Jesus tells the Twelve not to take any money or extra clothes. They have no plan and no map. They just have to take the risk, trust in their faith, and see what happens.

- How is that like your life? How is that unlike your life?

Jesus does tell them to take a walking stick—to support them as they journey.

- What gives you support? Do you have a hobby or an activity that gives your life structure and helps you to find meaning?

For Children

Jesus tells his friends to go on trips, two by two, and to tell everyone the Good News about Jesus. They can't take any money or any extra food, and they have no map or plan. They just bring walking sticks.

- Does that sound like an easy trip to take or a hard trip? Why?
- Why would they need walking sticks?
- How would you feel if you went on a trip with no money or extra clothes? Would you feel worried about what would happen to you? Would you wonder about what to do if you became hungry or dirty? What do you think Jesus' friends worried about?

Closing

No matter how much I probe and prod,
   I cannot quite believe in God;
But, oh, I hope to God that He
   Unswervingly believes in me.

(Rhymes for the Irreverent)

Sixteenth Sunday of the Year

23 July 2000
20 July 2003
23 July 2006

Jesus Calls Us to Rest

Scripture

- *Jeremiah 23:1–6.* The shepherd who misleads the sheep and scatters the flock will be punished. God will appoint good shepherds to care for the people so none will be driven away.
- *Ephesians 2:13–18.* Paul tells us that Jesus broke down barriers and brought people together; he replaced the old laws with one new law of love and peace.
- *Mark 6:30–34.* Jesus urges the Apostles to come away and rest after they return from their travel and ministry. They get in a boat to escape the crowd, but the crowd still finds them. Jesus sees those in the crowd as sheep without a shepherd; he gives in to the crowd and teaches.

Theme

Jeremiah tells the people God's idea of a good shepherd: one who cares for the people so they do not tremble and fear. As a good shepherd, Jesus urges the Apostles to get the rest they need, yet when the crowds catch up with them, he is moved by their need for a shepherd. Paul describes Jesus as the person who brought unity to the believers by his words and actions. In the Gospel story, Jesus demonstrates what Paul describes, as well as what Jeremiah foretold.

Focusing Object

A pillow

Reflections

For Adults

Jesus is always being a good shepherd, attending to the needs of people. He realizes his Apostles need rest, and they try to get some by taking a boat to a deserted place. But when they arrive, the place is anything but deserted! Jesus also recognizes the needs of the people who want to hear him speak to them and comfort them, so he lets the Apostles rest a bit while he does the talking for the time being. Jesus is flexible, and he shifts his focus when he sees that he is needed.

- Being a good parent, a good caretaker, or a good leader involves a sense of responsibility. Jesus urges his followers to rest when he sees their fatigue; he speaks to the crowds when he sees their hunger for the Good News. When have you seen the needs of others and attended to them? What is that like for you? Do you sometimes feel good about your caretaking? Do you sometimes feel resentful?

- Being a good parent, caretaker, or leader also requires flexibility. Jesus changes his plans when he reassesses the situation. How easily do you change your plans? How easily can you adjust when things don't turn out the way you expect?

- Jesus is usually good about getting the rest he needs. He is often described as going off to find a place to be alone and rest and pray. In this story he is doing it for the sake of others. Do you always get the rest you need? Do you urge others to get the rest they need?

- We live in a culture with such a hectic pace that quiet time often is not valued. What is the relationship in your life between getting rest and quiet time and feeling calm and confident? What is the relationship between feeling tired and feeling stressed and hassled?

For Teenagers

Jesus is so popular, he can't get away from the crowds. He tries to take the Apostles away in a boat for a little break, but the people find out where they are going, and they arrive ahead of the boat. Still, Jesus pities them and gives in to the crowd. He shifts his focus from resting to preaching. He begins to teach them with the words they long to hear.

- Who is someone you would follow with that kind of determination? Is there an athlete, a rock star, or some other performer or celebrity that you would want to see that much? Would you ever take another route to meet up with him or her, just to get a front-row seat? Why or why not?
- Would you like to be that famous? Would you like to draw such huge crowds that wherever you go, you have to take a pillow and do your sleeping in the car, boat, plane, or train? Would you like to be so popular that whenever you arrive anywhere, a crowd of fans is waiting to see you and hear from you? Why or why not?

The Apostles had just gotten back from a long journey and were telling Jesus about it. He urges them to get the rest they need.

- The teenage years can be a very busy time. Often lots of school, church, and community activities fill a young person's schedule. Is your life hectic? Do you get the rest you need? Do you get sick sometimes (or often) because you don't take care of yourself? Or do you eat nutritious meals, exercise, and get enough sleep? What do you think of the pace of your life?

For Children

Everyone loves Jesus. He tries to get away with his friends by taking a boat to a place to rest, but all these people follow him there because they love him so much.

- Do you think they had any pillows on the boat so they could rest?
- Do you think they still felt tired when they arrived and saw all those people waiting for Jesus?

- If you were there to see Jesus, would you have given him a pillow and let him rest? Or would you have wanted to talk with him and ask him questions and tell him things, also?
- Instead of resting, Jesus talks to the crowd of people. Why do you think he did that, even though he was tired?

Closing

You must shift your sail with the wind. —An Italian proverb

(Go for the Gold)

Seventeenth Sunday of the Year

30 July 2000
27 July 2003
30 July 2006

Jesus Feeds a Multitude

Scripture

- *2 Kings 4:42–44.* The prophet Elisha takes twenty barley loaves from a servant and gives them to a crowd of a hundred. Everyone eats and is satisfied. Some is left over.
- *Ephesians 4:1–6.* Paul reminds us that there is one faith, one Lord, and one baptism. He calls us to unity and peace, asking us to be patient and loving with one another.
- *John 6:1–15.* Jesus feeds a crowd of over five thousand with five barley loaves and two fish. Everyone eats and is satisfied. Twelve baskets of pieces are left over.

Theme

At this point in the cycle of readings, we have a shift from the Gospel of Mark to the Gospel of John. But this week there is no lack of continuity. The story of Jesus feeding the five thousand is the very next story in Mark's Gospel, following last week's reading. In fact this story appears in all four Gospels, and an additional story about Jesus feeding a crowd of four thousand appears in Matthew's and Mark's Gospels as well. Elisha's miraculous feeding is a foreshadowing of Jesus' miraculous feeding. The humility, meekness, and patience that Paul speaks about in the second reading certainly can be found in a person who would give up a personal lunch in order to feed a crowd.

Focusing Object
A lunch box, or a sack lunch

Reflections

For Adults

This well-known story is often linked to the Eucharist. The way Jesus takes the bread, gives thanks, and passes it to others to eat is very similar to what he does at the Last Supper. It's possible in both settings that the people present did not comprehend the depth or profound significance of the event in which they participated.

- Have you attended any event or experienced any situation that brought you only a delayed understanding of its significance? Has there been a time when you looked back with regret, thinking, "I wish I had realized at the time how important that moment was"? What happened? How did you eventually learn the greater significance?

The Apostles are in favor of dismissing the crowd of people into the local villages so they will be able to get some food for themselves. But Jesus calls them to a bigger challenge. He asks them to bring to him all that they have, and to trust that what they have to offer will be enough for what the people need.

- When have you been in that situation? When have you been faced with such a challenge—doubting your abilities, being asked to give your all, and needing to trust that doing your best will be enough? What happened?

For Teenagers

Who has the courage to bring forth those five barley loaves and two fish? A young person! It is a young person who makes the decision to share personal food with a crowd of people. That young person gives us an example of how we should be. That one young person makes a difference.

- Have you ever been in that situation? Have you ever done something that served as an example to adults as well as to other young people? If so, what did you do? What happened?

So often we want to make a difference, but we feel as if we cannot. "I am only one person. How can I make a difference?" is what we often ask ourselves. But most major changes in the world happen because one or two people have the courage to try something new.

- Have you ever tried something new? Have you ever had a dream about doing something different or starting a movement that might bring about a major change in people's behavior or attitude? If so, what is it? If not, what do you wish you could accomplish?
- If you had been the only person in a hungry crowd who would admit to having brought any food along, would you have offered it to Jesus so it might be shared with more than five thousand people? Why or why not?

Lots of times we try something new and it fails. At that point we have two choices. We can either give up or we can try again in a way that applies our learning from the first failed attempt. Sooner or later we will make a discovery: we will discover the right way to do something new, or we will discover that we've put enough time and energy into a difficult quest and it's time to change gears and focus on something else.

- Have you ever failed at some attempt, then learned enough to try and try again until you finally succeeded? If so, what happened?
- Have you ever failed at some attempt, tried again a few times, and finally decided that it was time to stop trying and to move on with something else? If so, what happened?

For Children

Jesus is talking to a lot of people. They are hungry by the end of the day, but they don't seem to have any food to eat. It is a young person who first offers to share food. And because of that one young person who shares one lunch box of food, the entire crowd of people is able to eat.

- If Jesus asked you to share your lunch with a big crowd of people, how would you feel? Would you feel afraid? Why? Would you feel proud? Why? Would you feel selfish? Why? Do you think you would give your lunch to Jesus? Why or why not?

- What do you think that young person thought when Jesus was able to take one lunch box of food and turn it into enough food to feed all those hungry people? What would you think if you had been there?

Closing

God makes three requests: Do the best you can, where you are, with what you have, now.
—African American folklore

(Acts of Faith)

Eighteenth Sunday of the Year

6 August 2000
3 August 2003
6 August 2006

𝔍esus, the
𝔅read of Life

Scripture

- *Exodus 16:2–4,12–15.* The Israelites are starving in the desert after their exile from Egypt, and God sends them manna—bread—to eat every morning.
- *Ephesians 4:17,20–24.* Paul tells us that believing in Jesus means giving up your old self for a new self, because our life is so different once we know Jesus. We become new people.
- *John 6:24–35.* Jesus challenges the people's faith, and they ask for a sign like the manna that Moses and their ancestors received in the desert. Jesus tells them that he is the bread they need for life.

Theme

Our faith is forever calling us to be new again. The Israelites have to become new people and live in a completely new way while they are in the desert. Followers of Jesus have to see themselves in a completely new way as they begin to match their life up to the standards Jesus has for them. Paul tells it like it is—we must lay aside our former self and embrace a fresh, new spiritual self.

Focusing Object
A piece or loaf of bread

Reflections

In the beginning of this Sunday's Gospel, the people ask Jesus how he has arrived there at Capernaum. The Scripture passages between last Sunday's Gospel and this Sunday's Gospel tell the rest of the story. Jesus flees to the hills and mountains and doesn't return by nightfall. So the Apostles get back into the only boat that is there (the boat they came in), and they head for Capernaum. The people who were fed that evening know that Jesus wasn't in the boat when the Apostles left, and they know there is only one boat. The next day a few more boats come to the shore, and some of the people take those boats to Capernaum. When they find Jesus there, they are puzzled. So it is a legitimate question to ask, "How did you get here?" What they don't know is that Jesus joined the Apostles in the boat in the middle of the night—by walking on the water.

- Jesus was a very puzzling character. And the crowds of people didn't know the half of it! Jesus' Apostles were constantly amazed at the miracles Jesus performed, and didn't know what to make of it all. But they trusted him, and they stayed with him. Have you ever been puzzled by a situation, yet you have trusted it and stuck it out, even though you couldn't necessarily explain why you trusted? What happened?

- Jesus knew these people were interested in his miracles, and some of them were not understanding the full impact of his words. He advised them to stop their search for perishable food and to focus on what is eternal. Do you do that? Do you focus mostly on the eternal? Or do you find yourself in the same rut of being overly concerned with the trappings of materialism, fads, and luxuries? How so?

- The people demanded from Jesus a sign like the manna from the desert. But they had just witnessed the multiplication of loaves! Do you ever miss the obvious in your relationship with Jesus?

Do you ever ask for a blessing, all the while not realizing the blessings you do have? How so?

For Teenagers

The people ask Jesus for a sign, like the manna-bread that Moses and their ancestors received in the desert. Jesus tells the crowd that he himself is the "bread of life."

- How strong is your faith? Do you feel connected to Jesus and believe he is present to you? Or do you wish you could have more miraculous signs—perhaps like bread falling to you from the sky?

Jesus recognizes that the people are more concerned with perishable food to fill their stomachs. He urges them to be concerned with the food that will not perish, with food that is eternal and that feeds the soul, not just the body.

- No one will deny that food for the body is necessary. But most of us never think about eternal food for the soul. What feeds our soul? What feeds yours? What helps your faith? What or who gives life to your relationship with Jesus? What or who helps you believe? How are you a person who brings "food for the soul" to others?

- Teenagers seem to be preoccupied with the latest fashion statement, the kinds of pants and shirts that are in style, the music that is currently topping the charts, and even the words and phrases that are popular in teen language. These are all fads that come and go, certainly like the "perishable food" Jesus talks about. What would Jesus say about teenagers and their love for these things? What do you think about them?

For Children

The people ask Jesus for a miracle, for something that can prove to them that God is with them. Jesus wants them to know that he himself is a miracle; he is God. So when Jesus is with them, God is with them.

- It was hard for some of the people to believe that Jesus is God. It was easy for others to believe in him. Do you believe that Jesus is God? Why or

why not? If you believe in Jesus, is it easy for you
to believe? Or is it hard?

- Jesus performed so many miracles for the people
  that it's hard to imagine why they didn't believe
  in him. Can you think of any of Jesus' miracles?
  If he came into this room and we could actually
  see him and talk with him, what miracle might
  you ask him to do? Do you think he would do it
  for you? Why or why not?

Closing

Evangelization is one beggar telling another where
he found bread. —D. T. Niles

(Action 2000: C Cycle)

Nineteenth Sunday of the Year

13 August 2000
10 August 2003
13 August 2006

Food for the Journey

Scripture

- ○ *1 Kings 19:4–8.* Elijah is exhausted, and tells God he is giving up. He asks God to take his life. But instead an angel comes and brings him a hearth cake and a jug of water. After eating, he walks for forty days and forty nights.
- • *Ephesians 4:30—5:2.* Paul tells us to imitate God, to follow the way of love.
- • *John 6:41–51.* Jesus tells us that he is the living bread come down from heaven.

Theme

Elijah is exhausted and ready to give up. But an angel brings food and drink to nourish him for his journey. Jesus is telling the crowds that he is their food for the journey. His flesh and blood are all the food we need. Paul tells us to forgive one another and to love others the way Jesus loves us.

Focusing Object

A jug or glass of water and a small loaf or cake

Reflections

For Adults

Elijah is exhausted after a real ordeal. He has proposed a challenge to the prophets who worship idols: Each of them is to prepare wood to sacrifice a bull, but not light the fire. Each of them is to pray to their god for the fire to start. Naturally the idol worshipers cannot light their fire. But even though Elijah has water dumped all over his altar, a fire starts as soon as Elijah prays to God. The king's wife is furious and threatens to kill Elijah the way he killed the idol-worshiping prophets, so he flees. This is the point where the first reading picks up. Elijah is so tired of his ministry, he wants to give up and die. But God gives him what he needs—he rests, eats, and drinks, and he is ready for the journey ahead of him.

- Elijah's life is in danger because of his faith. What inconveniences or discomfort have you suffered for your faith? Do you think you would be courageous enough to risk your life for your faith? Why or why not?
- What are today's modern idols? What seems to be worshiped by the common culture? What luxuries, trappings, or attitudes have become more important than God?
- When have you become burned out like Elijah? What brought you out of it? From what or whom did you find support and encouragement? What was the journey you had to walk?
- Everyone has but one life's journey. Elijah was ready to give up his, but God had more in mind for him to do. What do you hope to accomplish during your one life journey?

For Teenagers

Elijah is exhausted and ready to give up. He asks God to take his life.

- Have you ever felt that way? If so, what were the stresses and pressures that led you to that point? How did you get through it? If not, do you know anyone who has felt that way? Can you imagine being in that situation? What would you do?

Elijah doesn't want to take care of himself. He just wants to die. But an angel tells him to take care of his bodily needs or he won't have the strength he needs for the journey ahead.

- Do you take good care of yourself? If so, how? If not, why not? Do your parents ever encourage you to take better care of yourself? What do they tell you? Does it makes sense? Do you follow their advice? Why or why not?

God has big plans for Elijah, who already has done so much work telling people about God. And God is there for Elijah, helping him out when he doesn't know what to do or where to go.

- Do you think God has big plans for you? Why or why not? What might God's plans be for you? What are your plans? Do you think your plans will ever get in the way of God's plans? Do you think God's plans could ever get in the way of your plans? Why or why not? How can someone figure out what plans God has in mind for their life?

For Children

Elijah is a special holy man that always does what God asks him to do. But Elijah becomes too tired to go on, and he just wants to die. God sends an angel to bring him food and drink. Suddenly Elijah is strong enough to do God's work again.

- When do you get tired? What kinds of activities make you tired?
- How do you feel after you eat a good meal?
- What would you say if you were tired and hungry and an angel showed up with a special meal for you? Would you be happy or afraid? Why? What meal would be your favorite one for an angel to bring?

Closing

I expect to pass through this world but once; any good thing therefore that I can do, or any kindness that I can show to any fellow creature, let me do it now; let me not defer or neglect it, for I shall not pass this way again. —Attributed to Etienne de Grellet

(Familiar Quotations)

Twentieth Sunday of the Year

20 August 2000
17 August 2003
20 August 2006

Bread and Wine, the Flesh and Blood of Jesus

Scripture

- *Proverbs 9:1–6.* Wisdom invites us to a heavenly feast, with grand food and drink. We are asked to leave foolishness behind so we might advance in understanding.
- *Ephesians 5:15–20.* Paul urges us to be thoughtful and wise, and not to be foolish or ignorant.
- *John 6:51–58.* The one who eats the flesh and blood of Jesus is the one who lives forever.

Theme

Foolishness and ignorance will get us nowhere. The Proverbs urge us to eat and drink from the table of wisdom; Paul encourages us to be thoughtful and not to act like a fool. It takes faith and wisdom to understand Jesus' difficult words. This is the third Sunday with a Gospel passage about Jesus as the bread of life. The people listening to Jesus are still having a hard time believing and comprehending what he says.

Focusing Object

A glass of wine and a piece of bread

Reflections

For Adults

It's easy to see why people struggle with Jesus' words. How are they to know what Jesus means when he says that people must eat his flesh and drink his blood in order to live forever? Even with the insight of the Last Supper and the sacrament of the Eucharist, we struggle with the fullest meaning of these words.

- It is a central teaching of the Catholic church that the bread and wine of Communion (thought to be unchanged chemically or physically in any way) are indeed the body and blood of Jesus in the most literal sense. How easy or difficult is it for you to accept and understand this teaching? How might you explain it to a Christian of a Protestant faith denomination who sees Communion as a symbolic meal, and not necessarily as the real presence of Jesus?

- What is it like for you to worship at liturgy and receive the Eucharist? When you attend Mass, are you involved in "full, active, and conscious participation"? When you attend Mass, do you sometimes daydream and lose track of what is happening? Does liturgy play a major or a minor role in your prayer life and your relationship with Jesus? How so?

For Teenagers

When Jesus speaks of being the bread of life from heaven, the people listening probably don't understand what he is talking about. At least we understand what he did at the Last Supper, and how his real presence comes to us in the form of bread and wine at Mass.

- If you could ask Jesus to explain the sacrament of the Eucharist in terms that a teenager could relate to, what do you think Jesus would tell you?

- What is it like for you to go to Mass? Do you find Mass to be a spiritual experience and an important form of community prayer in your life? Why or why not?

- If you could give special training to priests on how to help the community celebrate Mass in a way that would involve and engage young people, what suggestions or advice would you give?

For Children

Jesus tells us to eat his body and drink his blood. That's what we do when we go to Mass and receive Communion. The bread we eat and the wine we drink has become the body and the blood of Jesus, even though it stills looks and tastes like bread and wine.

- Are you old enough to receive Communion at Mass? If you are, what is it like? Do you remember your First Communion? What was it like? Were you excited or afraid or happy that day? Did you have a special celebration at home?
- If you aren't old enough to receive Communion at Mass, do you know when you will be? What do you think it will be like? Are you looking forward to receiving Communion? Why or why not?
- What's it like going to Mass? Does someone help you understand what's happening at church? Do you sing the songs and say the prayers with all the people? Do you know the names of your priests at church? Does someone else at church help to teach you about Jesus? What is that person's name?

Closing

We don't know how to celebrate because we don't know what to celebrate. —Peter Brock
(Acts of Faith)

Twenty-First Sunday of the Year

27 August 2000
24 August 2003
27 August 2006

Serving God

Scripture

- ○ *Joshua 24:1–2,15–17,18.* Joshua gives the choice of loyalty to the tribes: "Whom will you serve?" He also announces the clear choice he and his family have made: they will be serving God.
- • *Ephesians 5:21–32.* Husbands and wives need to love and respect each other.
- • *John 6:60–69.* Many find Jesus' words too challenging; it is too difficult to follow him. Jesus gives the choice of loyalty to his Apostles.

Theme

God has always been faithful and loyal to us. The question is this: Will we be faithful? Joshua directs that pointed question to the tribes of Israel. They choose to follow the God who led them and their ancestors out of Egypt. Jesus asks that pointed question as well. Simon Peter's famous reply is, "To whom shall we go?" In other words, there is no one else to follow. Paul asks husbands and wives to be loyal and faithful to each other the way the church is to be faithful to Jesus. Loyalty and faithfulness start in the home, with the family.

Focusing Object

A house

Reflections

In Joshua's culture men are the only independent citizens. Women and children are seen as the property of men; the wife and children go along with whatever decisions the man makes. So when Joshua proclaims his own personal allegiance to God, he speaks for his entire household and family in the same breath without question. He does not need to consult with individual family members for clarification. It isn't so easy in our modern culture. Children often disagree with the religious beliefs and practices of their parents.

- When you were a child, did you disagree with any of the religious (or even political) viewpoints of either parent? Was this disagreement open and discussed, or was it secret and not discussed? What was that like? Have your and your parent's viewpoints grown more similar over the years or not? What is that like for you now?

- If you are a parent of a preteen, a teenager, or a young adult, how do you deal with disagreements regarding faith and religious beliefs and practices? If you are a parent of older adults, how did you deal with disagreements when your children were younger?

- If you are a parent of a younger child, what are some of the customs and habits you practice at home in order to pass on the faith to your children?

- If you are not a parent, do you see a difference in faith styles between young people and adults? If so, try to describe it. Do you think this difference is healthy and positive, or do you thing it is problematic? How so?

Although women in our country can vote, hold high-ranking positions, and live independently, women still have a long way to go before they are actually equal with men—in pay, opportunities, status, and privileges. And women in many other countries are still considered to be property. It is clear that greater changes are necessary. Yet women's rights, or the women's movement, can still be a very uncomfortable topic for both women and men to discuss.

- Why do you think discussing this topic creates such awkwardness?
- When are you most aware of the unfair disadvantages experienced by women?

For Teenagers

When Joshua tells the tribes of Israelites that he and his family have chosen to serve the one true God, he is able to speak on behalf of his wife and children. In his culture children and women are property. Whatever the husband and father says, the wife and children have to agree with.

- Do you disagree with any of the opinions that your parents have? Do you and your parents have the same preferences in the area of religious beliefs and practices? Or do you have different styles of faith and prayer? If there are differences, how are they dealt with at home?
- Do you think that life would be simpler, better, and easier if all children were required to agree with their parents and go along with whatever they say? Why or why not?
- When children disagree with parents, what are some respectful and courteous ways to communicate with parents and discuss important issues? How can children and parents get along and deal with huge differences that can separate them and cause negative feelings?

For Children

Joshua's family loves God, and they tell all the people of Israel that they will live the way God wants them to live.

- Do you think people in your family love God? How can you tell?
- How do you think God wants you to live? What kinds of things do you think God wants your family to be doing?

• If your family had to stand up in a big crowd and tell everyone that you love God and want to live the way God wants you to live, how would you feel? Would you be scared to talk in front of so many people? Would you feel proud to tell everyone that you love God? Would you be nervous? Would you want to do it or not? What would it be like?

Closing

The ruin of a nation begins in the home of its people. —An Ashanti proverb

(Acts of Faith)

Twenty-Second Sunday of the Year

3 September 2000
31 August 2003
3 September 2006

Purity
of Heart

Scripture

- *Deuteronomy 4:1–2,6–8.* Moses tells the people that the commandments they have will make them a great nation. The commandments will assist them in living carefully, with wisdom and intelligence.
- *James 1:17–18,21–22,27.* Listening to God's word is not enough. One must act on it, or the time spent listening is wasted.
- *Mark 7:1–8,14–15,21–23.* Jesus is criticized by the Pharisees and scribes because his followers do not observe the strict cleaning rituals of Jewish Law. Jesus criticizes these experts because they focus too much on rituals to avoid becoming "unclean." They need to focus more on attitudes and actions that come from the heart; those are what truly make us clean or unclean.

Theme

Moses wants the people to blend the spirit of the law with the letter of the law. Following the Commandments is important because of the effect it will have on the people. They will be better people because of the choices they make. Jesus makes a distinction between the letter of the law and the spirit of the law. Those who criticize him are far more concerned with the letter of the law—following the cleansing rituals in order to remain ritually clean. Jesus is more concerned with the spirit of the law—doing those things that are virtuous and avoiding those things that are sinful. Anything else is hypocrisy. We cannot become "unclean" from anything we touch or eat. Our cleanliness (or uncleanliness) comes from the inside. James emphasizes a similar point. Acting on the word makes all the difference. We know we are doing what God wants when we take action, and not when we merely hear about the action we ought to be taking.

Focusing Object
A cup or a pot

Reflections

For Adults

These experts of church Law are missing the point, and Jesus comes right out and calls them hypocrites. They are more concerned with rituals for outer cleanliness, yet less concerned with their own inner cleanliness. In an even more direct criticism (Matthew 23:25–26), which doesn't ever appear in the Sunday Gospel readings, Jesus tells these experts that they spend time washing only the outside of their cup, yet the inside remains dirty.

• How much time do you spend tending to outer cleanliness? How much time do you spend tending to inner cleanliness?

• For many people the appearance of having it all together is more important than actually having it all together. Without meaning to, how might we be passing that message on to our children and young people?

• Which rituals in your life are truly empty and meaningless? Which rituals are meaningful and symbolic and powerful in your life?

For Teenagers

Jesus emphasizes the purity that is in our hearts and the purity reflected by our actions. The people criticizing him emphasize the appearance of purity and the cleansing rituals required by Law in order to avoid becoming "ritually unclean."

- How much time, money, and energy is invested in cosmetics, hair products, fashionable clothing, and the like—just so we have the appearance of being popular and successful? Can any of these products actually make someone a better person? How so? What would Jesus say about our addiction to these products?
- As a society and a culture, do you think we are more interested in actual success or in the appearance of success? What is your definition of success?
- How much energy or effort goes into making ourselves better people? What opportunities are there for people to address what's on the inside of a person? What steps do you take (or can you take) to improve yourself from the inside out?

For Children

Jesus wants us to know that who we are on the inside is more important than what we look like on the outside.

- Who do you think makes Jesus happier: people with blue eyes, people with brown eyes, people with green eyes, or people who use their eyes to see what they can do to help someone?
- Who do you think makes Jesus happier: people with big hands, people with small hands, or people who use their hands to reach out and do good things for others?
- How can Jesus know if we love him? Is it by the clothes we wear? Is it by the color of our hair? Is it by looking at how tall or short we are? How can Jesus tell?

Closing

Things are seldom what they seem.
Skim milk masquerades as cream.
  —Sir William Schwenck Gilbert

(Success Every Day)

Twenty-Third
Sunday of the Year

10 September 2000
7 September 2003
10 September 2006

**The Deaf
Will Hear**

Scripture

- *Isaiah 35:4–7.* The prophet tells about the day when the blind will see, the deaf will hear and speak, the lame will leap, and waters will burst forth from the desert.
- *James 2:1–5.* If we treat the rich better than the poor, then we are discriminating and not following the way of Jesus. All of us are brothers and sisters.
- *Mark 7:31–37.* Jesus brings hearing and perfect speech to a man who is deaf and has a speech impediment.

Theme

The day Isaiah spoke about has come to pass. With Jesus those miracles are possible. Jesus reaches out to those in need, those society shuns, and he embraces them and brings them healing and wholeness. James warns us to treat all people well, as Jesus did, even those who seem to have lower status.

Focusing Object
A bell

Reflections

This is one of Jesus' miracles that amazes the people who are gathered. Despite Jesus' requests to not tell anyone what took place, the people spread the word quite freely and confidently. Jesus not only demonstrates miraculous powers but he pushes the cultural envelope by attending to the needs of a person with a disability. He also is establishing himself as the Messiah foretold by the prophets.

- James and Mark both challenge us to push the envelope of social customs and expectations and reach out to those who are not as elegant, not as well-esteemed, and not as privileged as ourselves. How do you do that in your life? How can you make that more of a priority? What are the concerns and risks involved with taking such action?

- Do you have any friends or relatives who are deaf? Do they use sign language? If so, do you know sign language? If not, how does that affect your ability to communicate? If you yourself are deaf, what is it like not hearing in a world built for those who can hear?

This story appears only in Mark's Gospel. That is significant only because most of what is in Mark's Gospel appears elsewhere, most often in Matthew and Luke. In fact it is believed that Mark's Gospel was the first Gospel written, and that both Matthew's and Luke's Gospels were written using Mark's Gospel as a source and guide.

- The Gospels are actually quite different in their details, despite their obvious similarities in theme and content. Do you ever compare versions of the same story by the different Gospel writers? Have you ever read one entire Gospel, start to finish, like a novel? (Mark is the shortest—it's a good one to start with!) How do you view the Gospels— as separate versions of the same reality? as four novels? as four sets of separate articles? as the same story told from four different perspectives?

- How did you become involved with reflecting on the Sunday readings? What motivated you to use this book or to join a prayer or discussion group? How does reflecting on the Sunday readings affect your experience of Sunday worship?

For Teenagers

People are amazed that Jesus can cure deafness. They are probably also amazed that Jesus would even be interested in giving any attention to a person who cannot hear. In his culture it was a popular belief that if you were deaf or blind or disabled in any way, it was because of a sin—your own sin or the sin of your parents. Anyone with such a condition was considered a social outcast, but Jesus is modeling a new type of behavior. He reaches out to anyone and everyone—even the ones most people are afraid to touch or talk to.

- What makes someone a social outcast in your school? (Please do not name any names, but discuss the traits or criteria that might be used to decide why a person might be given such a status.)
- Who decides who the social outcasts are? Is there complete agreement, or do different people have different ideas of who is acceptable and who is not acceptable? Does everyone know their own status? Is everyone aware that they are cast as acceptable or not acceptable? If so, how do they know?
- What would Jesus say about the social games that are played out by young people in their schools and in their circles of friends? What advice would Jesus give you? Are you willing to follow it? Why or why not?
- Do you have any friends or relatives who are deaf? Do you know any sign language? If you yourself are deaf, what is it like not hearing in a world built for those who can hear?

For Children

Jesus met a person who wasn't able to hear, and Jesus cured him. He was then able to hear and to speak clearly.

- Do you know anyone who is deaf? If so, does he or she use sign language?
- Do you know any sign language?
- What do you think would be the hardest part about not being able to hear?
- If you are deaf, what do you think is the most difficult thing about not hearing, and living in a world where most people can hear?

Closing

The bell rings loudest in your own home. —A Yoruba proverb

(Acts of Faith)

Twenty-Fourth Sunday of the Year

17 September 2000
14 September2003
17 September 2006

Service,
Carrying
the Cross
of Jesus

Scripture

- *Isaiah 50:4–9.* This is one of the Suffering Servant Songs, which is heard during Holy Week every year in the Wednesday weekday liturgy. It is seen as a foretelling of Jesus and his eventual suffering.
- *James 2:14–18.* Faith is useless unless it is reflected in good works. We need to pair our beliefs with actions; unless it is put into practice, faith is useless.
- *Mark 8:27–35.* Peter has the insight to see Jesus as the Messiah, but lacks the insight to know that Jesus must suffer, and that everyone must take up their cross and follow.

Theme

James tells us that faith that isn't put into practice is worthless. Peter has faith that Jesus is the Messiah, but he doesn't realize yet that putting his faith into practice means taking up the cross and following. Isaiah gives us a hint of what that following might be like.

Focusing Object
A blanket, a can of soup, and a cross

Reflections

For Adults

James is very practical. He wants us to see exactly what our faith is for. It's not for thinking, it's for doing. We must not merely wish our poorer brothers and sisters well; we must not merely pray for them. It is not enough. We must fill their bellies with food, we must cover their shivering bodies with clothing and blankets. Otherwise our faith is useless.

- This passage is direct and strong. James does not beat around the bush here. What is it like for you to have your responsibility to poor people spelled out in such a clear and challenging way?
- Where are the opportunities for you to be of service to hungry, homeless, and poor people? What are some things that you do or that you could be doing?

In the Gospel Peter goes from being the top dog to being in the doghouse. He is the one to declare that Jesus is the Messiah. In Matthew's version of this same conversation (Matthew 16:13–19), Jesus is so happy with Peter's response that he tells Peter that he is the Rock and that he is given the keys to heaven. This passage is seen as indicating that Peter was selected by Jesus to be the first pope. Yet just a few verses later, Jesus is calling Peter "Satan." Quite a switch.

- Obviously Jesus has seen Peter at his best and at his worst. Jesus has praised him when he's succeeded and forgiven him when he has failed. Whom have you seen at their best and at their worst? Who has seen you that way? Whom have you praised for successes and forgiven for failures? Who has praised and forgiven you? Is there anyone you cannot forgive?
- What does it mean to take up your cross and follow Jesus? When in your life have you had a sense of what that journey is truly all about?

In the second reading, James says it's not enough to pray for homeless and hungry and poor people. We need to give them food to eat and clothes and blankets to keep them warm.

- Do you think James means this literally? Do you think this means that even teenagers need to find ways to make the world a better place for people who don't have the same advantages we have? Why or why not?
- What opportunities are available for teenagers to serve the needs of the poor? How can you help? How can you make a difference?

In the Gospel Peter goes from the top to the bottom in no time. He scores high when he answers that Jesus is the Messiah, but then he gets reprimanded by Jesus when he doesn't want to hear of death and suffering. It's like a roller coaster ride for poor Peter.

- Have you ever had one of those roller-coaster days—up one minute, down the next? Describe what it was like. Do you think Peter could relate to that day? Can you relate to Peter's?
- Obviously Jesus loves Peter, even when he messes up. He congratulates Peter when he does well, and he criticizes him when he does poorly. Peter is praised when successful, and forgiven when unsuccessful. How is Peter's relationship with Jesus like your relationship with your parents? How is it different?
- Jesus speaks of following him and taking up the cross. He means that we will have to endure the suffering and the difficult times if we are to be his followers. Have you endured some hard times? Who has endured those hard times with you? When have you supported someone else going through hard times? Do you think this is what Jesus is talking about? Why or why not?
- How is taking up the cross and following Jesus (mentioned in the Gospel reading) connected to putting your faith into practice (mentioned in the

second reading)? How is Jesus' message similar to James's message?

For Children

Peter says one good thing to Jesus and one bad thing. Jesus is happy with the good thing, but he is unhappy about the bad thing. Yet Jesus still loves Peter.

- Do you sometimes say good things and sometimes say bad things? What do you say more of—good things or bad things?
- When you say good things, are your parents happy? How do you know? What do they say or do?
- When you say bad things, are your parents unhappy? How do you know? What do they say or do? How do you know they still love you?

Closing

If you want to see the brave, look at those who can forgive. If you want to see the heroic, look at those who can love in return for hatred. —*The Bhagavad-Gita*

(*Families Creating a Circle of Peace*)

Twenty-Fifth Sunday of the Year

24 September 2000
21 September 2003
24 September 2006

The Last
Shall
Be First

Scripture

- *Wisdom 2:12,17–20.* The wicked are generally jealous of the good; instead of affirming the goodness and imitating it, the wicked are shamed and want to destroy it.
- *James 3:16—4:3.* Disputes are caused by envy and selfishness; but wisdom is innocent, kind, and peaceable.
- *Mark 9:30–37.* Instead of discussing Jesus' words about his being put to death and then rising, the Apostles are discussing which of them is most important. Jesus teaches them that in order to be first, one must be last of all and servant to all. Whoever welcomes a child welcomes God.

Theme

The Book of Wisdom explains why Jesus was put to death: the wicked cannot tolerate goodness; they are shamed and threatened, so they seek to destroy it. James echoes the same theme when he says that quarrels happen when people envy what they cannot acquire, and their inner cravings make war. Yet wisdom cultivates peace, and the harvest is justice. The Apostles are not cultivating peace in the Gospel reading; instead they are arguing over who is "number one"—quite the opposite from what it takes to be number one, according to Jesus.

Reflections

Jesus is speaking about his death, and his rising on the third day. The Apostles don't understand what he is talking about, but they are too afraid to ask him. Instead they begin to pass their time arguing about which one of them is "number one." (At least they know enough to be embarrassed when Jesus asks them what they have been discussing.)

- When have you known enough to be embarrassed about something you said or did?
- When—in a less humble stage of your life, no doubt—have you not even known enough to be embarrassed about something you said or did until much later, after you grew up a bit?

Jesus says the only way to be the first is to be the last. The only way to be number one is to not try so hard to be number one.

- Our culture has become a culture that truly measures winning and losing. Just one or two generations ago, children played all kinds of games in back lots or yards near their home. Teams changed every day, and so did the rules and even the sports. Now we have organized sports leagues with teams and uniforms and coaches for even the youngest children. Instead of focusing on the playing, the focus is now on the winning. We have basketball camps and soccer camps for all ages, even for the very young. What is your view of this trend? Have you or your children or anyone you know participated in such leagues or camps? Do you think this focus always raises children's self-esteem? What attitudes have you observed in parents, coaches, and children?

At every football or baseball or basketball game, you can see them—the giant hands with the index finger pointing up, and the rest of the fingers curled together. They usually say "number one."

- Jesus says if we focus on being number one, then we certainly are not number one. If we try to say we are the best, or the most important, or the greatest, then we truly are not. If we do our best to not brag but to serve everyone else's needs and to build up everyone else's confidence, that is the way to true stardom. How hard is it to be that way when the culture urges us to be number one? How would Jesus handle it if he were a teenager at your school this year? Can you follow his example? How? Why or why not?

Many teenagers report that they have more fun being members of intramural teams than they do on a varsity or junior varsity team. They play more often, receive less criticism, and are under less pressure that way.

- How is that preference related to the message of this Gospel?

If the goal is to always win and be the number one team, then most players fail, because there can only be one number one team in whatever sport, league, or district you participate in; only one team can win. Everyone else loses. But if your goal is to learn, to put out the best possible effort, to improve, and to have fun, then everyone can succeed; everyone wins. The score doesn't matter. No one loses.

- How is this philosophy of sports related to the Gospel message?
- Could this philosophy of sports ever work in the professional area? Why or why not? In the high school area? Why or why not? In the grade school area? Why or why not?
- Where does money enter into the picture? How is money connected to the current philosophy of sports? What would Jesus say about this connection?

For Children

Jesus says the best way to be the best is to help everyone else become their best.

- Is there a sport, game, or hobby that you enjoy? Is it more fun alone or when you do it with someone clsc?
- Have you ever helped anyone get better at that sport or game or hobby? Has anyone ever helped you? What was that like?

Closing

Keep company with those who may make you better. —An English saying

(Go for the Gold)

Twenty-Sixth Sunday of the Year

1 October 2000
28 September 2003
1 October 2006

A Cup of Water in Jesus' Name

Scripture

- *Numbers 11:25–29.* Joshua is concerned because two people who were not in their original gathering receive the spirit and are prophesying. Moses calms his fears and reassures him. The more prophets, the better! The more people bestowed with the spirit, the better!
- *James 5:1–6.* The wealthy have much to grieve—their garments will be moth-eaten, their harvest will rot, and even their silver and gold will corrode—all because their wealth has caused such suffering among the poor.
- *Mark 9:38–43,45,47–48.* John is concerned because a person not of their group is casting out demons in Jesus' name. Jesus calms his fears and assures him that anyone doing good in Jesus' name—even if it's just to give a cup of water—will be rewarded. Jesus also reminds us that nothing should be more important than entering into the Reign of God.

Theme

Both Joshua and John have the same concerns. Both Moses and Jesus have the same response. Don't be so worried! Don't be such an elitist! Anyone can serve. If good work is being done, please don't stop it. Let it happen; in fact encourage it.

James reminds us that the good work we don't do can hurt us. If others suffer from our lack of service, we will be held accountable for it.

Focusing Object
A cup of water

Reflections

For Adults

In Moses' time and in Jesus' time, people are concerned about being in the "in crowd." If someone not from our group is prophesying or casting out demons, they should be stopped, according to Joshua or John. Moses and Jesus disagree: Our circle is big enough to include even those who didn't begin with us. Do not stop the good work being done. How can it hurt us? It can only help us.

- Clearly Joshua and John were concerned about who was "in" and who was "out." Perhaps they were jealous, perhaps they were confused, perhaps someone else's ministry threatened their own idea of who and what they were. When has someone else's success bothered you and threatened your own security? Of what have you been jealous? How did you deal with it?
- Have you ever tried to exclude someone from joining your in crowd? Have you ever been excluded from someone else's in crowd? What happened?
- In your job, volunteer work, or other activities, do you have any competition? How do you view others who do the same kinds of things you do—as colleagues or as opponents?
- Did you ever make a choice not to give someone "a cup of water" because they were your competition? How did you feel about that decision?

For Teenagers

In both the first reading and the Gospel, the same situation occurs. Joshua and John are concerned because an outsider is doing the kinds of things they are supposed to be doing. Moses and Jesus reassure them: There is nothing to worry about. The more, the merrier. Do not be jealous or insecure.

- When have you been jealous of someone else? When has someone's actions, talents, accomplishments, or friendships worried you? When have you begun to feel concerned that someone else's success might make your success less important or impressive?
- When has someone shut you out of their circle of friends? What was it like? How did you deal with it?
- Have you ever tried to shut someone out of your circle of friends? Why? What was the problem? What happened?

Jesus says that whenever we give someone even just a cup of water in his name, we will have our reward.

- What do you think it means to give something or to do something "in Jesus' name"?
- Have you ever decided to serve Jesus in that way? What was that like?
- Have you had the opportunity to serve Jesus in that way but chose to put it off, or decided to do otherwise? What influenced your decision?
- Do you think most teenagers would see serving Jesus as a worthy goal or priority? Why or why not? If not, what do you think of that opinion? How is serving Jesus any different from making the world a better place?

For Children

Jesus tells us to take care of one another and to welcome anyone who wants to be our friend. Jesus says that even giving someone a cup of water is a good way to take care of them.

- How do you take care of people in your family? How do they take care of you?
- How do you make new friends?
- When was the last time you can remember giving someone a cup of water?
- When was the last time you remember someone giving you a cup of water?

Closing

You don't have to have a college degree to serve. You don't have to make your subject and verb agree. You only need a heart full of grace. A soul generated by love. —Martin Luther King Jr.

(Go for the Gold)

Twenty-Seventh Sunday of the Year

8 October 2000
5 October 2003
8 October 2006

Like a Child,
Accept the
Reign of God

Scripture

- *Genesis 2:18–24.* Adam and Eve are of the same bone and flesh.
- *Hebrews 2:9–11.* Jesus becomes a little lower than the angels in order to experience life as a human being, with all the joys and sufferings of human life, including death.
- *Mark 10:2–16.* As Jesus is teaching that a man and woman joined in marriage are no longer two but one flesh, some people are bringing their children to him to bless and touch. His disciples try to discourage this, but Jesus insists that they come to him. All must accept the Reign of God as a child does, or they will not be able to enter.

Theme

Man and woman are made for each other as perfect partners; when they marry they become one flesh. Their children are a gift and an example for us to follow, for they show us the way to the Reign of God. The human condition, with its two sexes that join physically in the creation of children, is a wonderful condition. Jesus was not ashamed to join us in this wonderful, human condition, and we are honored and gifted that he did so.

Focusing Object

A doll

Reflections

It is easy to imagine Jesus preaching to a group of adults, as small groups of children come running up to him for hugs and blessings.

- What is it about children that they should be our role models for entering into the Reign of God?
- Why do you think the Apostles had been scolding the people for bringing their children to Jesus?

Some churches have nurseries for small children, so the parents can attend Mass without the distractions that small children can bring. Other churches have "cry rooms" with glass windows and sound systems, so parents with small children can see and hear Mass, yet keep the disturbances away from the rest of the assembly. Still other churches have neither nurseries nor cry rooms; they welcome children of all ages in all stages of development and activity. This is a source of great conflict for some parish families, because people hold many different opinions on what should be done.

- What is your preference? Why do you see it as the best option?

Jesus is enjoying the presence of the children coming to him for hugs and blessings. He makes it clear that we must imitate children and become like them in order to enter the Reign of God.

- Obviously Jesus is calling us to not be childish but to be childlike. How do you see the difference between being childish and being childlike? What exactly are we being called to?
- Not all characteristics of children are good for older people to imitate, but many are. What are some children's habits we should not try to pick up? What are some ways of children that we should try to remember and imitate?

- Do you ever baby-sit younger children? If so, what is your favorite part and your least favorite part of that responsibility? If you have never baby-sat before, what parts do you think you might look forward to, and which parts would you not look forward to?

For Children

Jesus tells adults that they should be more like you—that they should be more like children!
- Do you think a lot of adults wish they could be children again? Why or why not?
- Do you like being your age, or do you wish you could be a grown-up? Why?
- What's the best part about being the age that you are?
- What's your favorite thing to do? Do you think most adults would like doing the same thing? Why or why not?

People are bringing their children to Jesus so he can give them hugs and blessings. But the Apostles try to stop them. Jesus tells the Apostles to let the children come to him because he loves them.
- When you picture in your mind these groups of children coming up to Jesus, how do they look? Are they walking up to Jesus or are they running? Are they afraid or are they happy? Do you think they are laughing? Why or why not? Do you think Jesus is laughing? Why or why not?
- Who do you think laughs more often—children or adults? Why?

Closing

If children live with criticism, they learn to condemn.
If children live with hostility, they learn to fight.
If children live with ridicule, they learn to be shy.
If children live with shame, they learn to be guilty.
If children live with tolerance, they learn to be patient.
If children live with encouragement, they have confidence.

If children live with praise, they learn to
appreciate.
If children live with fairness, they learn justice.
If children live with security, they learn to have
faith.
If children live with approval, they learn to like
themselves.
If children live with acceptance and friendship,
they find love in others.

—Dorothy Law Nolte
(Families Creating a Circle of Peace)

Twenty-Eighth Sunday of the Year

15 October 2000
12 October 2003
15 October 2006

Jesus and the Rich Young Man

Scripture

- *Wisdom 7:7–11.* The spirit of Wisdom is praised. Gold and silver and precious gems are not worth as much as she is; all riches come to those who love her.
- *Hebrews 4:12–13.* God's word is profoundly powerful. God is almighty and all-knowing. Nothing escapes God's awareness.
- *Mark 10:17–30.* A rich young man struggles with the need to give up his possessions and follow Jesus. He walks away sad. Jesus comments that it's easier for a camel to pass through the eye of a needle than for a rich person to enter the Reign of God.

Theme

In the first reading, Solomon tells us how one can give up all riches and material wealth in order to seek Wisdom, yet find riches beyond imagination because of seeking Wisdom above all else. In the Gospel Jesus tells how one must give up all riches in order to follow him and find the Reign of God in heaven, which of course will be far more glorious than all the possessions that have been given up. How can we give up things? Why must we give up things? The second reading gives the answer: It is the almighty and powerful way of God.

Focusing Object

A needle in a pincushion

Reflections

For Adults

Jesus tells us it is difficult for a rich person to enter into the Reign of God, to enter into heaven. When a person has all the influence and power that comes with wealth, it is easy to take luxuries for granted and to expect special treatment. It is easy to dismiss the needs of poor people and to assume that rich people deserve their wealth and poor people deserve their poverty.

- What is your attitude toward the luxuries you think are necessities?

These words of Jesus should send shivers down our spines. We are the wealthy of the world. How easy is it for us to pass into the Reign of heaven?

- What is our responsibility to our brothers and sisters who walk the streets looking for clothing, daily food, and shelter?
- What is our responsibility to all the children growing up without the benefit of childhood security and stability?
- What is the relationship between poverty and crime?
- If society as a whole would sacrifice its luxuries and spend its money instead on education and training and care for disadvantaged people, what could be the outcome? Would the riches and wealth of that new society far outweigh the riches and wealth first sacrificed? Why or why not?

For Teenagers

Jesus gives us some harsh words: If you are rich, don't count on getting into the Reign of God. Don't count on entering heaven. Don't count on receiving all the wealth and riches you are looking for.

- Are most teenagers you know more interested in making good money or in doing good things for the world? What are you most interested in?

- Do you believe that money can buy happiness? Do you think most teenagers would agree with you? Why or why not? What does society's behavior indicate?

We don't hear the name of this rich young man. The Gospel doesn't tell us that he went away, never to return to Jesus again. We don't know if he ever did sell his possessions and give the money to the poor, or if he ever came back to follow Jesus.

- What do you think happened to him?
- If you were telling this story, how would you write the ending? What would happen to this rich young man, and how would he spend the rest of his life?

For Children

Jesus meets a young man who has a lot of money. Jesus tells him to give his money to people who are poor, people who need it. Then the man just walks away sad, because he really likes his money. But we never hear the end of the story.

- Do you think this man really liked his money more than he liked Jesus?
- Do you think this man went away and did what Jesus said?
- Do you think this man went away, kept his money, and was sad for the rest of his life?
- Do you think this man went away, kept his money, and was happy anyway?
- If you were with Jesus when this happened, what would you have said to this rich man?

Closing

By the accident of fortune [one] may rule the world for a time, but by virtue of love and kindness [one] may rule the world forever. —Lao-Tse
(Random Acts of Kindness)

Twenty-Ninth Sunday of the Year

22 October 2000
19 October 2003
22 October 2006

Seeking Status in the Reign of God

Scripture

- *Isaiah 53:10–11.* One of the five Suffering Servant Songs of Isaiah, this reading is part of the first reading heard on Good Friday every year. It speaks of the faithful servant's need to understand that suffering for God will lead to glory in heaven, and it is also seen as a foretelling of the story of Jesus.
- *Hebrews 4:14–16.* Jesus is not only our high priest, and the divine Son of God, but also a human being, who intimately knows our human condition and understands our weaknesses and sufferings.
- *Mark 10:35–45.* James and John ask for the reward of glory beside Jesus, one to his left and one to his right. Jesus prepares them for the cost of that reward, and then tells them that the reward is not his to give.

Theme

James and John ask an unusual request of Jesus—they want places of honor and high status beside Jesus when he comes into his glory. Jesus tells them that the path to glory leads through great suffering, and like Isaiah's suffering servant, he will suffer for the love of many. Jesus spells out the fate of many of the believers—the martyrs who end up doing the same thing Jesus did—suffering and dying for love. In this way Jesus understands our most profound sufferings and pain.

Focusing Object
A pair of gloves, or cutouts of a left hand and a right hand

Reflections

For Adults

A famous saying warns us, "Be careful what you pray for, you may receive exactly what you request." James and John didn't know what they were asking for when they said they could handle following in Jesus footsteps all the way. They were told they would be given the work, but that they might not "get the credit." Jesus wasn't in charge of the seating arrangements in heaven.

- When have you asked for more than you realized? When have you been given a challenge you weren't ready for?
- James and John clearly were after the rewards; the suffering part was something they had not completely thought through. When was a time you had your mind set on a reward without thinking through the cost of that reward?
- Have you ever done a lot of work, only to watch someone else get the credit for it? Have you ever gotten credit for some work that someone else actually deserved more recognition for than you? How have you handled these situations?

For Teenagers

James and John each want to be the "main man" for Jesus. Clearly, they are trying to be "teacher's pets."
- Have you ever tried to become someone's favorite? What was the outcome?

As you can imagine, the others are upset that James and John are trying to make secret deals on the side in order to outrank the rest of the Apostles.
- Have you ever felt slighted by someone else's success at outranking you and becoming the favorite?

Jesus is onto their little scheme. He knows what they are attempting, and he tells them that wanting such high status is going to cost them.

- Do you think their scheme worked? Do you think Jesus favored them above the rest?
- Do you think they learned their lesson? What did they learn?
- What do you think the other Apostles learned from this situation?
- What do you think you need to learn from this situation?

For Children

James and John ask Jesus if they can become his two favorite friends. Then Jesus' other friends become angry and start an argument.

- Why do you think Jesus' other friends became angry with James and John?
- Do you ever argue with your friends about which one is the teacher's favorite? If you have any brothers or sisters, do you ever argue with them about which one of you is a parent's favorite? If so, what's that like? What would Jesus say about that?

Jesus told all his friends that they shouldn't try to become the most important person. Instead they should all try to become the most helpful person.

- What does it mean to try to be the most important person?
- What does it mean to try to be the most helpful person?

Closing

The way to get things done is not to mind who gets the credit of doing them. —Benjamin Jowett
(Go for the Gold)

Thirtieth Sunday of the Year

29 October 2000
26 October 2003
29 October 2006

Jesus Heals Bartimaeus

Scripture

- *Jeremiah 31:7–9.* This is a song of delight in the work of God, who will deliver the blind and the lame, who will turn their tears into joy.
- *Hebrews 5:1–6.* This passage quotes Psalm 20, verse 7, and Psalm 110, verse 4, which refer to King David. Like Aaron and like David, Jesus is called by God. Jesus is humble, and he does not claim greatness for himself but only follows the call.
- *Mark 10:46–52.* Bartimaeus, who is blind, calls Jesus "Son of David" and asks for pity. Jesus heals him, and he becomes a follower.

Theme

In the first reading, Jeremiah speaks of One who delivers the blind; in Mark's Gospel Jesus cures Bartimaeus's blindness. In Hebrews Jesus is compared to David; in Mark's Gospel Bartimaeus calls Jesus "Son of David." In Hebrews Jesus is described as not glorifying himself; in the Gospel he raises the social status of a beggar just by giving him attention and care. Jeremiah urges all to proclaim the praise of God; Bartimaeus responds by following Jesus.

Focusing Object

A pair of sunglasses

Reflections

For Adults

Jesus asks Bartimaeus, "What do you want me to do for you?" Jesus heals him, with the news that it was Bartimaeus's faith that was the cure.

- If Jesus asked you, "What do you want me to do for you?" how would you answer? How is it that your faith can also bring to you that which you ask for?

Just seven weeks ago, the Gospel story was about Jesus healing a man who was deaf. The first reading that Sunday was from Isaiah, and it foretold of the day when the blind would see, the deaf would hear, and the lame would leap. It was becoming clear that Jesus was the One to come, the One to heal the blind and the lame, the Messiah. If you turn to Mark's Gospel, you will see that the very next passage after today's reading is Jesus' triumphant entry into Jerusalem. Bartimaeus could have been there with him, waving palm branches and yelling praises. Three chapters later Mark's Gospel tells the story of Jesus' arrest.

- What happened to all those believers? What happened to the blind and the deaf people who were cured? What was their faith in Jesus based on? Why didn't they come forward and assist their leader who was being treated unjustly?
- What is your faith based on? When someone is treated unjustly, do you always come forward and assist? If so, how? If not, why not?

For Teenagers

Bartimaeus's popularity increases immediately with the attention he receives from Jesus. One minute the crowd is scolding him to keep quiet, the next minute they are reassuring him and urging him to go to Jesus.

- Jesus' gift to Bartimaeus is not only his sight but also his status in the community. By reaching out to the outcasts of society, Jesus brings general acceptance to them. How might you be able to bring general acceptance to the "outcasts" at your school? What would happen if those students seen as unpopular were suddenly being given sincere attention and friendship by popular students?

Bartimaeus's response to Jesus' healing is to become his follower. Jesus tells him, "Be on your way." Bartimaeus chooses then to follow the way of Jesus.

- If Bartimaeus had been given sight, and yet failed to recognize God's blessings in his life, would that have been much of a success story?
- You have been given many blessings by God. Do you always recognize your good fortune? Are you grateful to God for all you have? How are you a success story? What response would Jesus want you to give, as a demonstration of your thankfulness for all you have been blessed with?

For Children

Bartimaeus is a man who is blind. He comes to Jesus and says, "I want to see." Jesus heals him, and he is then able to see.

- Do you know anyone who is blind?
- Do you know what a Seeing Eye dog is? Have you ever seen one?
- Do you know what the braille language is? Have you ever seen anything written in braille?
- What do you think would be the hardest part of not being able to see?
- If you are blind, what do you think is the hardest part about living in a world where so many people can see?

Closing

Religion is not a way of looking at certain things. It is a certain way of looking at everything.
—Robert E. Segal

(Vision 2000: A Cycle)

Thirty-First Sunday of the Year

5 November 2000
2 November 2003
5 November 2006

The Commandments

Scripture

- *Deuteronomy 6:2–6.* Moses makes it perfectly clear to the people of Israel that their only God is One God, and that they shall love God with their heart, soul, and strength.
- *Hebrews 7:23–28.* Jesus is unlike any other high priest.
- *Mark 12:28–34.* The scribe asks Jesus about the most important commandment, and he answers, quoting the book of Deuteronomy, with the passage that is today's first reading. Jesus adds that the next important commandment is to love your neighbor as yourself.

Theme

This first reading is the *Shema,* the most treasured prayer of the Jewish tradition. You will find it on the doorpost of many Jewish homes. It means "Hear, O Israel!" In the reading it announces the great commandment of love. Jesus, our one high priest, shows us that love is more important than anything. Loving yourself, loving your neighbor, and loving God are connected. Loving your neighbor comes more easily when you can love yourself, and loving God is most easily expressed by loving your neighbor. Jesus and this scribe both appreciate each other's insights on love; it is obvious in the warmth of their conversation.

Focusing Object
A heart

Reflections

For Adults

In Matthew's version of this same story, the affectionate interaction between Jesus and the scribe is missing. Here in Mark's story, the scribe affirms Jesus and says, "Excellent, teacher!" and Jesus affirms the scribe by telling him he is not far from the Reign of God. In many situations the scribes are not on friendly terms with Jesus. They feel threatened by him, so they attempt to trip him up on his own words. No such attempt is apparent here.
- When have you felt threatened by someone because of his or her age, gender, background, or fame? Have you ever done something you later regretted because of that insecurity? What happened?
- Where have you seen friendly and affectionate interaction between people that surprised you? Where have you seen less-than-friendly interaction that surprised you as well?

In Matthew's version of this same story (Matthew 22:34–40), Jesus tells us that the second commandment is similar to the first commandment.
- How is loving yourself and your neighbor similar to loving God with all your mind, heart, soul, and strength?

For Teenagers

Jesus tells us that loving God completely, loving our neighbors, and loving ourselves are our highest commandments.
- How are all the other commandments based on these?
- Is it ever all right (not sinful) to do something wrong, if no one will ever know about it and no one will ever be hurt by it? How does committing

a sin—even a secret sin that is never caught—hurt you?

Every time you make a selfish decision, you teach yourself to be selfish. Every time you lie, you teach yourself to be dishonest. Every time you make a considerate decision, you teach yourself to be caring. Every time you make a moral choice, you teach yourself to have integrity. Every time you do the right thing, you feel more confident, you like yourself more, and you respect yourself more.

- If everyone understood these concepts, how would it change the world?
- Is it possible to know and understand these concepts, but to ignore them? What kind of decision would it be to ignore them? Why would someone do that?
- Whom do you respect? Why do you respect him or her?
- Do you respect yourself? Why or why not?

Jesus and this scribe seem to like each other. They affirm each other's words. It's hard to tell who's the teacher and who's the learner.

- Do you know a teacher who has a similar relationship with you? What is that relationship like?

For Children

Jesus tells us that the most important thing we can do is love. We need to love God, we need to love other people, and we need to love ourselves.

- Who are some people you love? How do you show them that you love them?
- Who are some people that love you? How do they show you that they love you?
- Do you love God? What are some ways you can show God that love?
- Do you love yourself? What are some ways you take care of yourself to show that love?

Closing

Don't listen to those who say, "It's not done that way." Maybe it's not, but maybe you will. Don't listen to those who say, "You're taking a big

chance." Michelangelo would have painted the Sistine floor, and it would surely be rubbed out by today. Most importantly, don't listen when the little voice of fear inside of you rears its ugly head and says, "They're all smarter than you out there. They're more talented, they're taller, blonder, prettier, luckier, and have connections . . ." I firmly believe that if you follow a path that interests you, not to the exclusion of love, sensitivity, and cooperation with others, but with the strength of conviction that you can move others by your own efforts, and do not make success or failure the criteria by which you live, the chances are you'll be a person worthy of your own respect.
—Neil Simon

(Go for the Gold)

Thirty-Second Sunday of the Year

12 November 2000
9 November 2003
12 November 2006

Generosity

Scripture

- *1 Kings 17:10–16.* Elijah tells a woman to bring him some bread, but she tells him she has nothing to bring. There is only enough flour and oil for one small portion for herself and her son. He tells her to make him something first, and not to worry, for her jar and jug will not go empty.
- *Hebrews 9:24–28.* Other priests enter into sanctuaries made by hands; Jesus, the ultimate high priest, entered into the heavens made by the Divine Hand. Jesus will come again.
- *Mark 12:38–44.* Jesus criticizes the scribes who are very showy in the way they pray and parade around in public, but who are very unjust in their actions. He praises the efforts of the widow who contributes two copper coins, which she cannot afford. Jesus says her donation is greater than that of the wealthy, who only gave of their surplus.

Theme

Two widows are the heroes of today's readings. It is a widow whom Elijah befriends and blesses with abundance. She didn't have any extra oil or flour, but she gave all she had to Elijah because she had faith in his words. It is a widow who gives all the money she has that shames the contributions of the richest ones. She gives because she has faith. In contrast, Jesus criticizes the hypocritical ones who claim to be holy, yet who act in the most unholy ways. Jesus knows how they will fare at the Second Coming.

Focusing Object
Two pennies, or an empty jug and an empty jar

Reflections

For Adults

Jesus calls us to give generously—give our last two pennies, give the last bit of oil and flour until our jars and jugs are empty. We are not to be arrogant and parade around as if we are God's favorites.

- These words are meant to shake us up and force us to examine our own habits of giving. Obviously we are not being asked to literally give away all our food so that our children starve. But how generous is Jesus asking us to be? What areas in your life is Jesus asking you to reconsider? Sometimes we don't give because we think our little bit won't help. What would Jesus say to that?

- In some ways we do give until we have no more left to give. At times this isn't what Jesus is asking of us either. Jesus remembered to take appropriate days of rest when he needed to, and he would expect us to take care of ourselves so we don't burn out. When have you taken care of yourself so that you might continue to take care of others who are depending on you? Did you feel guilty taking care of yourself? When have you not taken care of yourself? What were the consequences of that?

- Who is a person that seems to live today's lesson? Who gives generously, trusts that God will provide, but still remembers to take care of personal needs? Is this person a peaceful and content person or a rushed and hassled person? Describe him or her.

For Teenagers

Centuries ago a widow was a very helpless person. In those days men controlled the family wealth and property, and women received any status they had from the men who were their husbands. Bad luck was a sign of sinfulness, so when a woman was widowed, she had no one to take care of her, and society looked down on her. Yet in both the first reading and the Gospel, we are asked to imitate the faithful actions of a widow.

- Jesus often asks us to look at the outcasts of society in order to imitate their ways. What are some characteristics of today's social outcasts that we need to imitate? How would imitating them make the world a better place?

- Jesus often asks us to see through the hypocrisy of the wealthy. They act proud and important, but many of their personal habits are not what we want to imitate. What are some characteristics of today's rich and famous that we wouldn't want to imitate? What kind of lifestyles do some well-known athletes, rock stars, and actors lead? What would Jesus say about these people?

- On most teenagers' bedroom walls and locker doors, you will find posters of whom? What characteristics of these people are admired by teenagers? Why? What would Jesus say about the choices made by most teenagers? What do you say about them? How are you prepared to respond to this situation?

- Do you ever contribute money or time to a cause you believe in? If not, why not? If so, what do you do? How has it affected your life? How has it made the world a better place for anyone?

- Some people think, "I'm only one person so I can't really help." What response could you give to that excuse? What would Jesus say about that?

For Children

One widow only has two pennies to give, but she does her best to give. Another widow has only a little bit of oil in her jug and a little bit of flour in her jar, but that is enough. Jesus tells us to try our best, and to know that it will be enough.

- Do you go to school? If so, is it easy or hard for you? Do you try your best? Do you like school?

- What chores do you have at home? What are the jobs you take care of in your room, in the kitchen, in the bathroom, or in the rest of the house? Do you try your best? Are these chores or jobs easy or hard for you?
- Do you ever give pennies or other coins to the collection at church? If so, how do you know when it's time for the collection? What happens?
- Did you ever help an adult bake bread or a cake? If so, what was it like? Did you use flour and oil? Did you enjoy it?

Closing

I am only one; but still I am one.
I cannot do everything, but still I can do
    something.
I will not refuse to do the something I can do.
                                    —Helen Keller
                                    (Go for the Gold)

Thirty-Third
Sunday of the Year

**Ending
Times**

Scripture

- *Daniel 12:1–3.* This is apocalyptic writing describing the end of time. It refers to the resurrection of the dead and eternal life. The wise who have led others to justice will shine forever like the stars in the heavens.
- *Hebrews 10:11–14,18.* Other earthly priests need to perform their sacrifices at the temple day after day; Jesus offered one sacrifice (himself), and it never has to be repeated. Now he sits forever in glory.
- *Mark 13:24–32.* Jesus describes the end of time in very dramatic terms. All kinds of unusual events will take place in nature. But when will this happen? No human being knows; nor do angels know. Not even Jesus knows. Only *Abba,* God the Creator, knows.

Theme

Apocalyptic literature is a symbolic, powerful style that is meant to bring hope to the oppressed and to warn those who oppress. Its purpose is not so much to give specific predictions but to describe the future in terms that are familiar to people, terms that often describe glorious events of the past. Both Daniel and Mark use this style of literature in today's readings. Because the end of the liturgical year is upon us (a new year starts with the first Sunday of Advent; next Sunday is the feast of Christ the King, the last Sunday of the year), we are hearing about the end times. In Hebrews Jesus is also described in heaven as if waiting for the end.

Focusing Object
A picture of the sun and moon

Reflections

For Adults

Natural events in the heavens and on earth have always carried a sense of mystery, even in modern times when we have a clearer understanding of science. But imagine the concern of people centuries ago when there were solar eclipses, lunar eclipses, comets, earthquakes, and meteor showers. People naturally want to understand the rhythms of the earth, and Jesus in the Gospel reminds us that we watch the fig tree sprout to know that the sap is high and summer is near. So an upset in these natural signs can be worrisome. It seems that many Christian believers want to take literally the first part of this reading (that these signs signal the end of time), but they don't want to take literally the last part of this reading (that no one knows when the exact day or hour is). The bottom line is this: We cannot predict the end of the world.
- Do eclipses and comets and meteor showers intrigue you or upset you?
- Do you enjoy learning about natural science?
- Are you concerned when cults and doomsday prophets proclaim predictions for the immediate end of the world? How do you respond to such predictions?

For Teenagers

There is often a lot of talk and frenzy about the end of the world coming. It especially happens with certain natural phenomenon such as comets, eclipses, and meteor showers. It's important to understand that Jesus insisted we cannot know the day or the hour, that we cannot predict when this will happen.

Sometimes unusual events in the heavens are just natural phenomenon for us to enjoy, not to worry about.

- Do you worry about the end of the world? If so, why? If not, why not?
- When you hear talk about predictions of the end of time, how do you feel? What do you say? What do you think about?
- Do you ever worry about dying? If so, why? If not, why not?
- Are you interested in cosmic happenings—planet alignments, comets, stars, and the like? How so?

For Children

Jesus tells his friends about the day he will come back to earth, riding on the clouds.

- Jesus knew that his friends would miss him when he left and went back to heaven. Do you know anyone who died and went to heaven? Whom do you miss? What was that person like?

Jesus wants his friends to understand that he is the Special One sent by God. When he returns he won't just pull up in a car. He won't be riding a horse or a donkey. He'll be riding on the clouds!

- What would you think if you looked up and saw Jesus coming down from the sky in the middle of the clouds? Would you run and tell someone? Would you just stand there and watch? Would you hide? Would you yell, "Hi, Jesus"? What would you do?
- How would you feel? Would you be excited? afraid? happy? worried? proud to be able to see him yourself?

Closing

We return thanks to our mother, the earth, which sustains us.
We return thanks to the rivers and streams, which supply us with water.
We return thanks to all herbs, which furnish medicines for the cure of our diseases.
We return thanks to the corn, and to her sisters, the beans and squash, which give us life.

We return thanks to the bushes and trees, which
provide us with fruit.
We return thanks to the wind, which, moving the
air, banishes diseases.
We return thanks to the moon and stars, which
give us their light when the sun is gone.
We return thanks to the sun, which looks upon
the earth with a beneficent eye.
Lastly, we return thanks to the Great Spirit, in
whom is embodied all goodness, and who
directs all things for the good of all children.

—An Iroquois prayer
(Families Creating a Circle of Peace)

Thirty-Fourth Sunday of the Year (Christ the King)

26 November 2000
23 November 2003
26 November 2006

A Kingdom
Not of
This World

Scripture

- *Daniel 7:13–14.* This is apocalyptic literature expressing the glory of the Chosen One in the clouds of heaven, returning to the Ancient One at the end of time, when his dominion and kingship shall last forever.
- *Revelation 1:5–8.* This is also apocalyptic literature expressing the glory of Jesus, returning amid the clouds, ruler of all kings, who made us all a royal nation of priestly people in service.
- *John 18:33–37.* Jesus argues with Pilate over what kind of kingdom belongs to Jesus.

Theme

Jesus says that his kingdom is not of this world. He further says that he came into the world to testify to the truth, and that those committed to the truth will hear his voice. The apocalyptic readings from Revelation and Daniel certainly describe a king who is not limited to this world. But our main task as followers of Jesus and disciples of his way is clear: we are to work in order to bring the kingdom of God into this world. It will not be the kind of kingdom we often think of, with a dominating, oppressive ruler and cowering subjects. It will be a Reign of peace and love, forgiveness and nonviolence.

Focusing Object

A globe, or a world map

Reflections

For Adults

Jesus never calls himself a king. Pilate does. And the church does.

- Why do you think Jesus never referred to himself as a king?
- Why do you think the church does? Is it a good, descriptive title? Or can it be misleading? How so? "Thy kingdom come, thy will be done, on earth as it is in heaven."
- If our job is to bring the Reign of God to earth, here and now, what should be our focus? What is the purpose of our lives? How do we go about doing this? Where do you see yourself fitting into this purpose and plan?
- It takes courage to live in the Reign of God, because everyone else doesn't play by the same rules. When have you seen that courage in yourself? What makes it so difficult?

For Teenagers

Jesus tells his closest friends that he is the Messiah, the One chosen to come and lead Israel into a new way of life. Only, their idea of a messiah king is different. They are waiting for a Jewish political leader who will take over the nation and destroy their enemies, then persecute them the way the Jews have been persecuted by the political powers of their time. The ways of Jesus are different. He is a "king" of nonviolence, forgiveness, unconditional love, and service.

- How would this difference in the expectations of a messiah king affect the perceptions of Jesus' followers?
- How might it lead to them doubting that he is truly the Messiah?
- How might it explain their cowardice at the time of Jesus' arrest and trial?

The Lord's Prayer we pray at Mass every Sunday includes this line: "Thy kingdom come, thy will be done, on earth as it is in heaven."

- What does it mean for the Kingdom to come to earth, the same way it exists in heaven? What would that look like?
- What would the world be like if everyone on earth did the will of God?
- What part do you play in bringing to this world the Kingdom Jesus has in mind? Are you playing your part? If so, how? If not, why not?
- It takes courage to play your part. When have you done something courageous for the Kingdom of Jesus? What happened? When have you had the chance, but not the courage you needed? What happened?

For Children

Jesus is our king. If we want to live in the Kingdom of Jesus, then we need to do things his way.

- The way of Jesus is the way of love and forgiveness. When have you done something wrong and hurt someone? Did you say you were sorry and ask for forgiveness? What happened? Has someone ever hurt you? Did that person ask for forgiveness? What happened?
- The way of Jesus is the way of service and helping others. When have you helped someone? When has someone helped you? What are some ways you can do an even better job of being helpful?
- The way of Jesus is the way of peace and nonviolence. Jesus does not want us hitting, slapping, or hurting one another in any way at all. When you are angry, and you feel like hitting or punching someone, what is a better thing to do? What would Jesus want you to do instead?

Closing

I do not ask to walk smooth paths nor bear an
    easy load.
I pray for strength and fortitude to climb the
    rock-strewn road.

Give me such courage and I can scale the hardest
    peaks alone,
And transform every stumbling block into a
    stepping stone.

—Gail Brook Burket
(Go for the Gold)

Index by Theme

Theme	Scripture	Pages
Hebrew:		
Angel wakes Elijah, gives him water and food	1 Kings 19:4–8	83–85
Joshua announces that his house will serve God	Joshua 24:1–2,15–17,18	89–92
Jesus acts:		
God calls Samuel; Eli explains the call to Samuel	1 Samuel 3:3–10,19	23–25
James and John ask for right and left spot	Mark 10:35–45	119–121
Jesus and the Apostles try to escape crowds in boat	Mark 6:30–34	71–74
Jesus calls Simon, Andrew, James, and John	Mark 1:14–20	26–29
Jesus feeds crowd of five thousand	John 6:1–15	75–78
Jesus praises Peter for recognizing him as the Messiah; then calls him Satan	Mark 8:27–35	100–103
Jesus sends forth the Apostles in pairs	Mark 6:7–13	68–70
Jesus sends forth the disciples to baptize	Matthew 28:16–20	15–18

Theme	Scripture	Pages
First must be last and servant of all	Mark 9:30–37	104–107
Give a cup of water in my name	Mark 9:38–43,45,47–48	108–111
A house divided will not stand	Mark 3:20–35	51–53
I am the bread of life	John 6:24–35	79–82
Let the children come	Mark 10:2–16	112–115
The most important commandments	Mark 12:28–34	125–128
Mustard seed	Mark 4:26–34	54–57
New patches; new wineskins	Mark 2:18–22	43–46
Pilate questions Jesus	John 18:33–37	137–140
Prophet not accepted in hometown	Mark 6:1–6	65–67
Rich enter Reign of God as camel passes through eye of needle	Mark 10:17–30	116–118
Ritual cleaning will not purify the heart	Mark 7:1–8,14–15,21–23	93–95
Widow's two coins the most generous gift	Mark 12:38–44	129–132

Index by Focusing Object

Acknowledgments *(continued)*

The excerpts on pages 18, 74, 107, 111, 121, 127–128, 132, and 139–140 are from *Go for the Gold: Thoughts on Achieving Your Personal Best* (Kansas City, MO: Andrews and McMeel, Ariel Books, 1995), pages 136, 287, 234, 368, 276, 284, 18, and 281, respectively. Copyright © 1995 by Armand Eisen.

The excerpts on pages 22, 57, and 64 are from *Native Wisdom for White Minds: Daily Reflections Inspired by the Native Peoples of the World,* by Anne Wilson Schaef, PhD (New York: Ballantine Books, 1995), n.p. Copyright © 1995 by Anne Wilson Schaef.

The excerpts on pages 25, 29, 53, and 82 are from *Action 2000: Praying Scripture in a Contemporary Way: C Cycle,* by Mark Link, SJ (Allen, TX: Tabor Publishing, 1992), pages 137, 134, 167, and 154, respectively. Copyright © 1992 by Mark Link.

The excerpts on pages 32 and 35 are from *Mission 2000: Praying Scripture in a Contemporary Way: B Cycle,* by Mark Link, SJ (Allen, TX: Tabor Publishing, 1993), pages 257 and 154. Copyright © 1993 by Mark Link.

The excerpts on pages 39, 46, 50, 78, 88, 92, and 99 are from *Acts of Faith: Meditations for People of Color,* by Iyanla Vanzant (New York: Simon and Schuster, Fireside Book, 1993), n.p. Copyright © 1993 by Iyanla Vanzant.

The excerpts on pages 42, 67, and 124 are from *Vision 2000: Praying Scripture in a Contemporary Way: A Cycle,* by Mark Link, SJ (Allen, TX: Tabor Publishing, 1992), pages 213, 126, and 157, respectively. Copyright © 1992 by Mark Link.

The excerpts on pages 60 and 95 are from *Success Every Day,* by Weight Watchers (New York: Macmillan General Reference, 1996), n.p. Copyright © 1996 by Weight Watchers International.

The excerpt on page 70 is from *Rhymes for the Irreverent,* by E. Y. Harburg (New York: Grossman Publishing, 1965), page 1. Copyright © 1965 by E. Y. Harburg.

The excerpt on page 85 is from *Familiar Quotations,* 14th ed., by John Bartlett, edited by Emily Morison Beck (Boston: Little, Brown and Company, 1968), page 531. Copyright © 1968 by Little, Brown and Company.

"One of the unique characteristics of this book, along with reflections on the lectionary readings, is the inclusion of a focusing object. Besides lending insights into the Scriptures, the focusing object trains people to see symbolically. In doing so, it enhances the ability 'to see more than meets the eye,' to see the extraordinary in the ordinary, the sacred in the secular." **Dr. Maureen Gallagher**, Archbishop's Delegate for Parishes, Diocese of Milwaukee, Wisconsin

"Lisa-Marie is definitely 'in touch' with the needs of young people and families—and how they approach the word of God. *In Touch with the Word* will not only help various generations in praying the Scriptures, but will also assist homilists in making the word come alive in their preaching." **Thomas N. Tomaszek, MEd, MTS**, Director, Spectrum Resources, Milwaukee, Wisconsin, and consultant to the National Federation for Catholic Youth Ministry's Prayer and Worship Project Team